Scholastic
WORKSHOP

DRAMA

5 to 7

Published by Scholastic Ltd,
Villiers House,
Clarendon Avenue,
Leamington Spa,
Warwickshire CV32 5PR
Text © 1999 Alison Chaplin
© 1999 Scholastic Ltd
2 3 4 5 6 7 8 9   1 2 3 4 5 6 7 8

Author
Alison Chaplin

Editor
Clare Gallaher

Assistant Editor
Clare Miller

Series Designer
Joy White/Sarah Rock

Illustrations
Paula Martyr

Cover illustration
Sarah Kelly

Designed using Adobe Pagemaker

British Library Cataloguing-in-Publication Date
A catalogue record for this book
is available from the British Library.

ISBN 0-590-53825-X

Scholastic WORKSHOP

Contents

ACKNOWLEDGEMENTS

The publishers gratefully acknowledge permission to reproduce the following copyright material:

Clive Riche for 'The Princess Who Wouldn't Smile' by Clive Riche © 1999, Clive Riche, previously unpublished.
Tony Stone Images/Stuart Westmorland for the photograph on page 82.

Every effort has been made to trace copyright holders for the works reproduced in this book, and the publishers apologize for any inadvertent omissions.

This book is based on a content outline by Geoff Readman. The Glossary of Terms, Assessment chapter, the Discrete Activities and the project 'Storytelling and Making' is based on material also written by Geoff Readman. The project 'The Zoo Company' is based on an original project written and created by Eileen Pennington.

Alison Chaplin is the manager of 'Arts on the Move', a company specializing in providing training for teachers, which includes working with drama in primary schools.
For information call 0161 881 0868.

The author would like to thank Mr Ken Chaplin for kindly providing the photographs on pages 159 and 161 used in the project 'Interpreting History'. Thanks also to Geoff and Katherine Warburton of 'Q-ten' for their assistance in reproducing the photographs.

Chapter One

INTRODUCTION

WHAT IS DRAMA?

In the broadest terms, drama has always made an important and profound contribution to the growth and development of a society. Its origins and purpose stem from our human need to act out stories, create rites, take part in rituals and communicate our thoughts and feelings to others. This universal need is apparent in all cultures whenever humankind tries to reach new understanding of complex events, phenomena and personal experiences through the process of re-enactment. By using our imagination to create performance we seek to enhance our personal security and our understanding about the most extreme and fundamental dimensions of human experience: birth, peace, hope, oppression, famine, death, victory.

Drama in schools, with its processes of re-enactment, communication and sharing, is integral to cultural growth and individual development. It offers a powerful and unique learning process that enables children to formulate understanding of the world around them. The process can be as simple or as complex as the learning outcome requires.

Although some aspects of drama work will result in a performance or presentation, an 'end product' is not always necessary in productive and successful drama work. It may help to consider drama conventions as a learning *process*, and theatre (or performance) as a *product* of that process.

Much drama work in school is concerned with enabling children to participate in a shared experience; either exchanging ideas, thoughts and personal viewpoints, or simply experiencing the same activity. In drama, children often behave 'as if' they are someone or something else. This is known as role-play and often takes place within a defined context. The context, which can be imagined or real, is selected by teachers for its teaching and learning potential. A shared context helps children towards a shared learning aim or outcome, participating together in specific events and circumstances. Drama offers children safe and secure contexts in which to explore dilemmas and feelings. The shift in perspective that occurs during role-play creates a sense of critical and objective distance that in its turn enables effective experiential learning to take place.

WHY TEACH DRAMA?

Drama can succeed where other subjects fail. At its simplest, it enables children to develop understanding and awareness of themselves and of others. Drama conventions used with young children will implicitly build self-confidence, develop the ability to interact positively with others, improve verbal and language skills, develop listening skills, create a sense of 'group' within a disparate body, encourage appropriate responses and create awareness of both the immediate and the wider world around them.

Many primary teachers use drama strategies within their daily timetable of classroom activities. The essence of drama is present in many of the games, role-playing pursuits, movement exercises, and action songs and poems which are widely taught from nursery age onwards.

Drama can prepare children for learning in that it encourages development of cognitive skills, their ability to interpret, to question and to respond. Drama is non-restrictive – no child should feel excluded or unable to participate. It has no boundaries, retains no prejudice and enables every child to achieve. Used as a teaching tool to access and explore a variety of subjects, drama is a powerful, valuable and effective teaching process that stimulates and concentrates the thinking processes of its participants. Used as a discrete subject in its own right, drama is an invaluable facilitator of personal, social and educational development.

DRAMA IN PRIMARY SCHOOLS

Drama is a subject which has great diversity of form, technique, content and structure. Primary school children who are 'doing drama' may be engaged in any of a whole range of activities. For example, they may be:

- in role as market traders on a newly discovered planet, with the teacher narrating the story as they enact it
- reading a play text in groups, then discussing a moral dilemma arising from their reading
- performing a presentation of recent topic work at a school assembly
- acting out traditional rhymes or action songs
- performing a well-rehearsed operetta about the nativity story, in full costume, on stage with lighting and so on.
- interpreting a scene from a story using sound effects which they have created.

So what are the key conceptual features that are common to all drama work? Effective school drama work normally involves the following elements.

A specific learning objective

This identifies the precise learning outcome that the teacher wishes to achieve in a particular session. The objective may be shared with the children before or during teaching, or afterwards as they reflect on their work.

A clear context

The context is the fictional or imaginative location of the drama. All children need clear contexts for learning that harness their enthusiasm and encourage them to integrate new knowledge and skills with those they have already acquired from school and home.

Only this can ensure effective education – the real understanding based on deep learning that makes a difference to how children understand and operate in their world.

When children do not have clarity about the context they are working in, they naturally become confused and frustrated. It is the teacher's responsibility to ensure that the children know:

- where they are
- who or what they are
- when the drama is taking place
- what they are expected to do.

Scholastic Drama Workshop helps teachers select and develop specific aspects of drama craft within contexts that are exciting and meaningful and that encourage children to use their own knowledge and skills in new and powerful ways.

Appropriate roles

Role-play is central to 'as if' behaviour and is essential to the imaginative and empathetic nature of drama work. It may include movement and mime, reading text, making sounds, exploring issues or developing performance skills. It is the teacher's responsibility to select appropriate roles that enable children to participate fully in the drama work.

Scholastic Drama Workshop helps teachers to use role-play to direct, facilitate, narrate, guide or take part in drama work with children. It shows teachers how to make use of role as a powerful teaching strategy.

Dramatic form

Teachers and children need to be aware of certain key dramatic forms or strategies that are central to successful drama work. They also need to use an appropriate critical vocabulary to describe the drama concepts they are using.

Scholastic Drama Workshop gives teachers the subject knowledge they need in order both to select and use appropriate dramatic forms, and to use appropriate language to describe them. It helps teachers understand the value of working with drama strategies and how to harness their learning potential for teaching across the curriculum.

The 'Glossary of terms' (see pages 21–36) gives brief, clear and comprehensive definitions of specialist vocabulary.

Group interaction

Drama is a social activity and draws on the dynamics of participants. It is essentially a group activity. Even 'solo' activities such as mime or monologue usually either develop or lead into group activities. Those watching the drama, the audience, also interact with the drama activity as they respond and become involved in it.

Scholastic Drama Workshop's approach involves children in working with partners and in groups. It recognizes that children learn by working beside others who are intellectually and practically engaged in similar activities.

A problem or dilemma

Drama offers strategies that help children to examine problems and dilemmas from different perspectives. Dilemmas often involve children in making difficult choices and considering alternatives. Although not always essential for drama work to be effective, a dilemma gives it energy and purpose by motivating children to engage and participate in a given context.

The teacher's task is to select a suitable dilemma that focuses the drama work for the children, enabling them to engage and explore implications of their actions.

Scholastic Drama Workshop helps teachers to select dilemmas that have learning potential, and shows how through drama work, children can examine problems from different perspectives, consider choices and make decisions.

COMMON CONCERNS ABOUT TEACHING DRAMA

• **Drama is just 'messing about'; the children won't learn anything and they'll just run riot!**

This is a popular misconception about drama, probably arising from the noisy interaction which occurs in many lessons! Drama is a valuable learning method which, when properly structured and planned, is invaluable as a teaching 'tool'. Many drama lessons can be noisy and this has often been viewed as ineffective learning, but much of the noise arises from productive and positive interaction within the group. No teachers will intentionally allow their pupils to 'mess about' and drama teachers are no different in this respect! Children will learn a great deal due to the experiential nature of drama work, and will absorb far more information on a wide variety of curriculum subjects than with any other teaching method. It is also an excellent means of exploring PSE issues and can form direct links to literacy, music, history, geography and PE teaching, to name but a few! Methods of assessment can be facilitated through the *Desirable Outcomes for Children's Learning* and via various levels at Key Stages 1 and 2.

• **I don't have the time or space to teach drama.**

Drama isn't restricted to using a specific time or space. The conventions used for drama work can be utilized within any classroom context and lifted and discarded at any time. Drama can easily be included in any class-based lessons and particular methods chosen as another teaching approach for any subject, topic or issue within the classroom environment. Don't assume that all drama work has to be operated on a long-term, intensive basis and that therefore extra time and space have to be set aside. It's wonderful if you have hall time or a suitable area for more expansive drama work, but not essential.

• **I don't feel sufficiently skilled to use drama – you have to be a specialist, don't you?**

Most specialists would like you to believe that, but it isn't true! Many teachers, armed with knowledge, enthusiasm, an appreciation of the subject – and a little courage! – can use

drama effectively. Good planning and preparation are essential in order to maintain control, change direction if required and achieve lesson objectives. Be prepared to begin with the basics and build your skills and use of conventions slowly. Don't feel that you've failed if a lesson has to be abandoned; use the experience to plan future lessons more effectively. Reputable specialists are always available to provide training and support for teachers who are seeking to expand their drama skills, and always remember that primary teachers with special responsibility for maths, history or geography are not necessarily specialists in those subjects, yet teach them with ease!

• **Drama is putting on plays, isn't it? What about those children who are not strong performers?**

Drama isn't primarily about performing. Your wonderful end-of-term plays and Christmas productions are really 'theatre' – a product arising from drama work. The premise of drama is centred upon sharing, experiencing and communicating, and any child has the ability to do all three. A vast number of drama conventions do not even rely on the need for strong language skills and so are appropriate to any age or ability level. Many children will obviously emerge as 'natural' performers and therefore their contribution to any performance aspects of the drama work will be stronger, but all children will respond positively in some respect to the drama that they experience, regardless of whether this response is implicit or explicit.

HOW THIS BOOK IS ORGANIZED

This resource book aims to enable teachers to include drama as a regular entitlement for children throughout the school year. For teachers without previous drama teaching experience, it provides subject content knowledge and practical advice on how to start; more experienced teachers will find it consolidates their skills and helps them continue to develop their knowledge and experience.

It provides:

• a coherent framework to help teachers develop the quality of drama teaching and learning
• an assessment model for evaluating drama work
• a glossary of drama conventions
• progressive and developmental resources in the form of short, focused activity ideas that support the teaching of specific drama skills and strategies
• six structured drama projects, each with a particular subject focus and broken up into manageable sessions, which children work on over a period of time. (Although a specific year group is suggested for each project, this is not prescriptive. Some projects will be accessible to more than one year group in terms of context, drama conventions and curriculum aims.)

USING SCHOLASTIC DRAMA WORKSHOP

Scholastic Drama Workshop is a resource, not a scheme. The materials have been devised in the belief that it is the quality, content and appropriateness of the learning activities and the interactions between the teacher and the children that are important in teaching drama.

The Workshop approach

The Workshop approach does not reflect a particular form of classroom organization. It recognizes that drama is a practical and intellectually creative activity and that the challenge lies in doing it; that children learn

about drama through effort and enquiry. Indeed, it can be used with any classroom organization. Each teacher can and should decide how best to organize the classroom space and time.

Only the teacher can decide when children will benefit from studying particular drama strategies in depth. The activities in Chapter Four will help children to become aware of techniques they can, or maybe already, use. But children also need to experience a complete drama process. The longer projects detailed in Chapters Five to Ten are ideal for this. Some teachers will plan around a drama project, using the discrete activities in a fairly *ad hoc* manner as specific issues arise; others may prefer to plan focused teaching on a series of specific drama skills and intersperse a drama project within the class.

Where do I start?

This depends on the attitudes and needs of the class and how well the class and teacher know each other. The single most important thing that children require is a classroom ethos that recognizes the value of their ideas and provides a supportive, enthusiastic environment in which to learn.

- It is helpful if you are enthusiastic, motivated, imaginative and creative in order for the children to be so too!
- At the heart of productive drama work is discipline. For this reason, before embarking on any drama session, make sure you have clearly defined a plan, a structure, a learning objective, a context (where and when the drama is taking place), roles (who or what are the children and what are they expected to do?) and control of the class.
- Take time to establish the rules of participation so that children realize the need to listen, understand, negotiate, co-operate and collaborate with others.
- Ensure that the children are clear about the following informing principles: there is no 'right' or 'wrong' way to do drama; they should not feel embarrassed or uncomfortable in the contexts you select; drama draws on personal experiences,

beliefs and social strengths, so everyone's ideas are valuable; drama work relates to real issues and feelings.

- Work on whole-group exercises and methods until the rules are fully established.
- If practical, allow children the opportunity to observe others at work if they do not feel able to participate.
- Gradually tighten the focus of the drama work and expand the complexity of conventions you work with.
- Gradually reduce the group size and increase the degree of individual participation in order to build confidence.
- Empower children to take more control of their drama work as their confidence increases.
- Be prepared to stop the drama at any time and to pause if you feel things are slipping away from your control. Reassess and change direction if necessary. Don't view this as a failure but as an essential part of productive and successful drama teaching.
- If you want to introduce your class to drama conventions and to begin to create an atmosphere of trust, encourage appropriate behaviour and develop appropriate responses, consider how you use drama in your current teaching practice and build on those activities. Drama games and simple mimes, action rhymes and basic movement exercises are ideal methods of introduction. Use the glossary and Chapter Four to find drama ideas that suit your needs.
- Once you are more experienced and are ready for more extended work which approaches drama as a discrete subject, try the projects in Chapters Five to Ten. These projects encourage children to become highly involved and enthusiastic about their work. They allow the teacher to observe the children and to find out about their areas of interest and what they find easy or difficult.

Remember: drama is one of the most accessible ways of engaging children in safe and secure contexts, enabling them to make meaningful decisions, followed by appropriate analysis, reflection and response.

This quality in itself is sufficient reason for drama to permeate the subject structure of the primary curriculum, and for it to become an effective and essential teaching approach for all primary teachers.

Scholastic
DRAMA
Workshop

Scholastic
WORKSHOP

Chapter Two

ASSESSMENT

ASSESSMENT IN DRAMA

Assessment in drama is complex, but needs addressing if the subject is to have status and credibility in schools. The National Curriculum for England and Wales places Drama within AT1, Speaking and Listening. In Scotland, Drama is included within Expressive Arts, which has its own set of 5–14 National Guidelines. Where possible, reference is made to this document, but *the assessment framework offered here is the author's own* and is intended to be supportive, not prescriptive, providing a framework within which whole-school development can take place.

There are three key elements in the drama process. Each will vary in level of prominence, and may occasionally be difficult to identify separately when a child is fully participating in drama. They often overlap and combine. They are defined and categorized as:

- creating and planning (approximates to Scottish 5–14 Guidelines for Drama Outcome Expressing Feelings, Ideas, Thoughts and Solutions)
- engaging and performing (approximates to Scottish 5–14 Guidelines for Drama Outcome Using Materials, Techniques, Skills and Media)
- reflecting and analysing (approximates to Scottish 5–14 Guidelines for Drama Outcome Evaluating and Appreciating).

It is hoped that teachers and students will find the following level descriptors and statements of attainment reports useful for facilitating a whole-school policy, with the more specific assessment criteria helpful in weekly or project planning.

Level descriptions

Level 1 (approximates to Level A of Scottish 5–14 Guidelines for Drama): children demonstrate a perception and recognition of imagined experience. Individual ability to work in small and large groups varies considerably. There is a growing capacity to interpret stimulus material, to make suggestions and to discuss drama with others. The activity of watching drama is valued and there is a desire to comment and reflect upon the work of others. Drama conventions are beginning to be recognized.

Level 2 (approximates to Level B of Scottish 5–14 Guidelines for Drama): there is a growing awareness of the needs of others in drama and a capacity to respond within both small and large group structures. Events of the drama can be described and recalled, with alternative suggestions, both in and out of role, being presented clearly. The relationship between the pretence and reality is readily understood as it operates in a variety of drama conventions and narrative forms.

Level 3 (approximates to Level C of Scottish 5–14 Guidelines for Drama): pupils can plan, perform and respond in different contexts, employing drama conventions with some skill. Their developing critical vocabulary enables them to discuss the work of others objectively, and with a developing confidence. They are beginning to recognize some distinctive dimensions of performing and participating in drama and are able to discuss key themes and issues. They understand the importance of flexible groupings.

Level 4 (approximates to Level D of Scottish 5–14 Guidelines for Drama): pupils can plan, perform and respond in drama in an increasingly broad range of fictitious contexts and extended projects. They are able to sustain roles appropriately, and to adopt roles which benefit the needs and demands of the drama in a sensitive and purposeful way. Skills and techniques of performance are developing, with a growing ability to define meaning in drama form as it relates to audience needs. They are able to evaluate drama conventions and make suggestions about when and how they should be used.

Level 5 (approximates to Level E of Scottish 5–14 Guidelines for Drama): pupils can negotiate and implement drama forms effectively and can engage in drama conventions in both small and whole-group contexts. They recognize that drama involves exploring issues and understand the differing demands of performance and participation. They are able to define drama conventions, as well as employ them. They recognize and utilize the skills of performance and can define drama meaning in relation to particular genres. When reflecting, they are capable of posing alternatives, appraising the work of others and defining some of the elements of drama, such as symbol, role and tension.

Scholastic
DRAMA
Workshop

STATEMENTS OF ATTAINMENT IN DRAMA

Child's name _____ Date _____ Level _____

By the end of the **Nursery** stage, children should be able to:	Skills grade	Evidence and commentary	End-of-year comment
Planning and creating			
• create a fictitious context by using small world play			
• adopt roles within defined environments			
• accept a teacher's use of role			
• make relevant suggestions			
Engaging and performing			
• create narrative individually			
• re-enact storylines			
• begin to interact with teacher-in-role			
• join in drama routine such as mime, movement activities, games and action songs			
Analysing and reflecting			
• recall events from stories			
• explain what they are doing in drama			
• offer opinions about parts of the drama			

Skills grade
1 Has not demonstrated this skill
2 Has demonstrated this skill with considerable support
3 Has demonstrated this skill with some support
4 Demonstrates this skill consistently
5 Demonstrates this skill consistently and effectively

Signed _____ Date _____

RECEPTION/PRIMARY 1

STATEMENTS OF ATTAINMENT IN DRAMA

Child's name _____ Date _____ Level _____

By the end of **Reception/P1**, children should be able to:	Skills grade	Evidence and commentary	End-of-year comment
Planning and creating			
• play with peers and negotiate a fictitious location in play			
• adopt roles and create an environment			
• understand the learning contract relating to drama and reality			
• suggest songs, games and activities			
Engaging and performing			
• engage in dramatic narrative with a partner			
• interact with peers in an in-role context			
• engage with one or two conventions			
• display a willingness to participate in drama routines, games and action songs			
Analysing and reflecting			
• recall events, songs and rhymes and describe them			
• explain what they are doing and who they are in drama			
• express opinions about why they liked or disliked part of the drama			

Skills grade
1 Has not demonstrated this skill
2 Has demonstrated this skill with considerable support
3 Has demonstrated this skill with some support
4 Demonstrates this skill consistently
5 Demonstrates this skill consistently and effectively

Signed _____ Date _____

Scholastic
DRAMA
Workshop

YEAR 1/PRIMARY 2

STATEMENTS OF ATTAINMENT IN DRAMA

Child's name _____   Date _____   Level _____

By the end of **Year 1/P2**, children should be able to:	Skills grade	Evidence and commentary	End-of-year comment
Planning and creating			
• work with a partner in dramatic contexts			
• adopt specific roles and create a dramatic environment			
• work within the learning contract relating to drama and reality			
• recognize the basic drama conventions			
Engaging and performing			
• adapt to a variety of fictional roles			
• interact with teacher-in-role in whole-group dramas			
• present ideas through drama conventions			
• participate in individual, small-group and whole-group drama contexts			
Analysing and reflecting			
• recall the events and the decisions from the drama			
• present a personal viewpoint			
• offer critical comments			

Skills grade
1 Has not demonstrated this skill
2 Has demonstrated this skill with considerable support
3 Has demonstrated this skill with some support
4 Demonstrates this skill consistently
5 Demonstrates this skill consistently and effectively

Signed _____   Date _____

Scholastic
DRAMA
Workshop

STATEMENTS OF ATTAINMENT IN DRAMA

Child's name _____ Date _____ Level _____

By the end of **Year 2/P3**, children should be able to:	Skills grade	Evidence and commentary	End-of-year comment
Planning and creating			
• plan in pairs and small groups			
• take responsibility for creating roles			
• negotiate and contribute specific ideas relating to drama and reality			
• suggest some conventions to direct the drama			
Engaging and performing			
• adopt and sustain fictional roles			
• interact with both teachers and peers in role			
• present ideas in a chosen dramatic form or convention			
• utilize space and movement in a variety of groupings			
Analysing and reflecting			
• recall, describe and evaluate events of the drama			
• suggest alternatives from a personal viewpoint			
• appraise some of the drama of their peers			

Skills grade
1 Has not demonstrated this skill
2 Has demonstrated this skill with considerable support
3 Has demonstrated this skill with some support
4 Demonstrates this skill consistently
5 Demonstrates this skill consistently and effectively

Signed _____ Date _____

Scholastic
DRAMA
Workshop

YEAR 3/PRIMARY 4

STATEMENTS OF ATTAINMENT IN DRAMA

Child's name _____   Date _____   Level _____

By the end of **Year 3/P4**, children should be able to:	Skills grade	Evidence and commentary	End-of-year comment
Planning and creating			
• negotiate and plan in small and large groups			
• respond and plan roles from a stimulus			
• respect alternative viewpoints in both drama and reality			
• work with drama conventions with minimal teacher support			
Engaging and performing			
• adopt, sustain and create fictional roles			
• negotiate meaning with teacher and peers-in-role			
• present ideas within a range of drama conventions			
• use language, space and movement to communicate to others			
Analysing and reflecting			
• describe, recall and analyse the events of the drama			
• suggest alternatives and analyse the drama			
• reflect on key effective moments in the drama			

Skills grade
1 Has not demonstrated this skill
2 Has demonstrated this skill with considerable support
3 Has demonstrated this skill with some support
4 Demonstrates this skill consistently
5 Demonstrates this skill consistently and effectively

Signed _____   Date _____

STATEMENTS OF ATTAINMENT IN DRAMA

Child's name _____ Date _____ Level _____

By the end of **Year 4/P5**, children should be able to:	Skills grade	Evidence and commentary	End-of-year comment
Planning and creating			
• negotiate and plan in small and large groups			
• in groups, listen to, respond to and interpret stimulus material			
• respect and value the views of peers and include them, when appropriate, in the drama			
• work on self-initiated tasks and utilize drama conventions			
Engaging and performing			
• adopt, sustain and create a variety of fictitious roles			
• negotiate and interpret meaning with peers and teacher-in-role			
• engage and present ideas within a comprehensive set of drama conventions			
• sequence drama for performance			
Analysing and reflecting			
• describe the events, moods and issues of the drama			
• analyse and present different viewpoints of the problems of the drama			
• analyse key drama moments and say why they are effective			

Skills grade
1 Has not demonstrated this skill
2 Has demonstrated this skill with considerable support
3 Has demonstrated this skill with some support
4 Demonstrates this skill consistently
5 Demonstrates this skill consistently and effectively

Signed _____ Date _____

STATEMENTS OF ATTAINMENT IN DRAMA

Child's name _____ Date _____ Level _____

By the end of **Year 5/P6**, children should be able to:	Skills grade	Evidence and commentary	End-of-year comment
Planning and creating			
• through discussion, arrive at whole-class and small-group decisions to focus the drama			
• listen to, respond to and interpret a variety of stimulus material			
• utilize the ideas of others in creating effective drama			
• work on self-initiated tasks and purposeful drama conventions			
Engaging and performing			
• adopt, sustain and develop a variety of fictitious roles			
• sustain a role with the rest of the class for an extended period of time			
• engage and respond to a full range of drama conventions			
• sequence, present and perform in a variety of ways			
Analysing and reflecting			
• define and debate the issues of drama			
• evaluate the drama experience and suggest alternative action			
• define the techniques being used and appraise the performance of others			

Skills grade
1 Has not demonstrated this skill
2 Has demonstrated this skill with considerable support
3 Has demonstrated this skill with some support
4 Demonstrates this skill consistently
5 Demonstrates this skill consistently and effectively

Signed _____ Date _____

YEAR 6/PRIMARY 7

STATEMENTS OF ATTAINMENT IN DRAMA

Child's name _____ Date _____ Level _____

By the end of **Year 6/P7**, children should be able to:	Skills grade	Evidence and commentary	End-of-year comment
Planning and creating			
• negotiate whole-class and small-group decisions to focus the drama			
• interpret and make a considered response to stimulus material			
• value diversity of opinion in creating effective drama			
• demonstrate their understanding of drama elements, such as tension and symbol, in drama conventions			
Engaging and performing			
• adopt, sustain and develop roles to give the drama momentum and focus			
• sustain and develop a role with the rest of the class for an extended period of time			
• engage in and suggest a full range of conventions			
• create effective drama sequences for performance, which reflect tension and symbol			
Analysing and reflecting			
• reflect and define the meaning of the drama			
• suggest alternative dramatic action and take responsibility for it			
• recognize performance techniques, including the use of tension and symbol, in appraising the work of others			

Skills grade
1 Has not demonstrated this skill
2 Has demonstrated this skill with considerable support
3 Has demonstrated this skill with some support
4 Demonstrates this skill consistently
5 Demonstrates this skill consistently and effectively

Signed _____ Date _____

Scholastic
DRAMA
Workshop

Chapter Three
GLOSSARY OF TERMS

A GLOSSARY OF DRAMA CONVENTIONS

Drama conventions, or methods, are an identifiable range of activities which are used in the planning, executing, experiencing, performing and evaluating of any drama work. Much of the drama work contained in the discrete activities (Chapter Four) and the projects (Chapters Five to Ten) is centred upon the application of various established drama methods. Drama conventions have therefore evolved through regular use into recognizable and accessible processes which give the subject credibility and status. They:

- give children and teachers an appropriate, succinct and critical vocabulary for dramatic activity
- enable non-specialists to understand the key dimensions of drama as a creative process and facilitate the identification of focus, tension, role and so on
- provide teachers with a structure and framework for drama lessons, which will immediately involve children exploring ideas, themes and concepts

- can be used with different age groups, from ages four to sixteen, so long as the learning aim is clear and the content is at an appropriate level
- develop skills, understanding and knowledge simultaneously
- can be used as teaching strategies within many curriculum subject areas.

The teacher's role and skill in terms of choice and use of appropriate conventions is essential, both in expressing the way a convention normally operates and occasionally in creating new conventions for a particular learning aim. This glossary describes some of the more commonly used conventions. It is organized using the following headings:

WHAT & WHY?
defines the convention.

HOW?
gives an example of how the convention might be used with five- to seven-year-olds.

RESOURCES
details appropriate resources for the convention.

Scholastic
DRAMA
Workshop

A DAY IN THE LIFE

WHAT AND WHY? A technique which explores stages or moments in a character's life, leading to a specific point in the drama. It can be approached through a reflective dramatization of how a particular dramatic moment was arrived at, or simply by the creation of a number of scenes which re-create the stages in a character's day. Either approach enables children to analyse and reflect on specific points in the drama, and allows moments of change or tension to be highlighted.

HOW? Children explore and re-create a typical day in the life of Little Red Riding Hood when 'away from the story', devising scenes which show her existence at home prior to the story's start.

RESOURCES None.

BRAINSTORMING

WHAT AND WHY? A quick-fire discussion process in which children express their immediate thoughts about a specific word, issue or subject. These thoughts are recorded on paper by either the children or the teacher and can be used as a point of reference in later work, or as a prompt at the beginning of following lessons. The main aim is to encourage children to respond quickly to suggestions from the teacher and, in doing so, to provide answers which are less cautious or guarded than they would be as a result of prolonged discussions.

HOW? The teacher sits among the children with a large sheet of paper and a marker pen and invites them to respond to the word 'friendship' by suggesting the thoughts, words, phrases and images which immediately come into their minds. The teacher records all of their ideas on the paper. These suggestions are then used to explore the concept of 'friendship' or to form the basis of work on bullying.

RESOURCES A3 paper and marker pen.

COLLECTIVE DRAWING

WHAT AND WHY?   A small group, or the whole class, create an environment or a situation by drawing a picture. This can be as simple, or as complex, as the teacher decides. As the group's thoughts and ideas are incorporated within the drawing, verbal statements (for example, about the issues in the drawing and their feelings about the drama context) can be useful additions, enhancing the children's commitment to the drawing.

HOW?   Children draw a picture of what they think the woods were like in *Little Red Riding Hood*.

RESOURCES   Card or paper of an appropriate size, colour and shape. Crayons, pencils or felt-tipped pens. Prepare materials in advance if you intend using this method in the middle of a lesson.

CONSCIENCE ALLEY

WHAT AND WHY?   The group or class form two, parallel-facing lines (the 'alley'). Each line has a contrasting viewpoint. A main character in the drama, who has to make a decision, walks down between the lines and each child has the opportunity to influence or persuade him or her to their point of view. Children should discuss and decide their viewpoint in advance.

HOW?   A chief walks down the alley. The two lines give advice about whether the chief should take his or her people into battle.

RESOURCES   None.

Scholastic
DRAMA
Workshop

DEFINING THE SPACE

WHAT AND WHY? Children arrange school furniture, PE equipment, cloths or other materials to represent fictional places in drama.

HOW? Small groups of children build an imaginary 'village' using PE equipment to show where their houses are, in preparation for a drama involving the 'Best Kept Village' competition.

RESOURCES Large cloths, blankets and ribbons can be very useful, as well as school furniture and PE equipment.

DIARIES/LETTERS/JOURNALS

WHAT AND WHY? These can be used in a number of ways: as a stimulus to start the drama; during the drama to provide additional information about the context; to create a problem or dilemma, or as a development of character or role; to enable reflection and to stimulate recall after the drama, or to provide a prompt for future drama work. They can also be introduced by the teacher-in-role to create a tension or to change the direction of the drama. All contributions can be written in or out of role.

HOW? A letter is used to introduce a drama: the teacher comes into the classroom and reads a letter from a king whose daughter wants a new and novel toy for her birthday. She has been lonely recently and he wants to make sure the toy is a suitable one. The king asks the children for their help. The children, in role as toy-makers, plan new toys and give advice to the king.

RESOURCES As available and appropriate. Store them carefully for future use.

DRAMA GAMES

WHAT AND WHY? Drama games are a whole-group approach for encouraging interaction, building self-confidence, establishing appropriate behaviour within the 'perimeters' of drama work, improving speaking and listening skills and stimulating appropriate responses. They will facilitate an environment of support, trust and encouragement, which it is essential to establish prior to initiating more in-depth work. Ensure that the games are purposeful by linking them to your proposed learning outcome and by asking the children to reflect on their learning achievements.

HOW? The class play 'Fruitbowl' (see page 44). In this game the children sit in a circle and swap seats each time a name of a fruit is called, each child having been allocated a different fruit name. Other categories, such as modes of transport (car, aeroplane, train, bus, for example), can be used to name the children instead of names of fruit. Children can also be asked to move across the circle in a specific way, for instance as an aeroplane or car if using a 'transport' theme.

RESOURCES Generally none, but occasionally as specified.

DRAMATIC PLAY

WHAT AND WHY? The enacting of a situation without a direct focus or dilemma. It does not have a specific structure and is closely akin to play.

HOW? Although the whole class may experience dramatic play at the same time, it often involves small group work. For example:
- family groups living in the same block of flats
- groups of chefs, cleaners or porters working in a large hotel
- families working on an allotment, planting new vegetables.

RESOURCES Dependent on the context. It may involve the use of chairs, tables, suitable props and so on.

Scholastic
DRAMA
Workshop

FORUM THEATRE

WHAT AND WHY?   A small group enacts a situation observed by the rest of the class in order to explore a dilemma or problem. The observers can stop the drama whenever they feel it is necessary, for example when there is a need for clarification of the performers' motives, actions or reactions. The observers can also be invited by the teacher to step into the action to replace existing performers, in order to add to the dialogue, explain a character's motive or help to move the action forward. The teacher is central to this convention, observing, guiding, questioning and organizing continuously. Forum theatre is quite a difficult convention to explore with very young children. It needs to be introduced simply, with perhaps two confident children performing a familiar dramatic context. It is easier if the teacher takes a role initially.

HOW?   Two children suddenly realize that they are lost in a large market. The rest of the class watch a short scene and then advise them on what to do next.

RESOURCES   As appropriate.

HOT-SEATING

WHAT AND WHY?   A group (as themselves) question or interview a teacher or child in role. This may happen during a drama – the action is paused and a particular character is questioned for further information. Alternatively, it may be used to start a drama, and when the children need to find out as much as they can about a character. It can also be used to introduce a topic or story. The teacher may take the 'hot-seat' to support participants. Indeed, it is often advantageous for children to see their teacher using this convention, as they will feel far more comfortable with this to begin with, until they are more familiar with what is involved.

HOW?   Children 'hot-seat' their teacher in a role taken from a storybook they are reading.

RESOURCES   A chair!

MASKS

WHAT AND WHY? Masks may be simply made or purchased commercially, and come in all shapes and sizes. They may cover the whole face or just the eyes, and could be made from card, paper or Mod-Roc, for example. Care should be taken to ensure total safety with mask work, particularly with children who are asthmatic. Once the masks are made, it is recommended that the children have time to experiment in small groups, and to discuss the impact, meaning and effect of wearing the mask. This convention is helpful in enabling young children to differentiate and sustain roles.

HOW? In a drama about legends connected with the forest, a group of children wear masks to represent the creatures of the forest. The rest of the class are explorers who observe the creatures and discuss their movements and appearance, hiding in the forest to avoid being seen.

RESOURCES Masks can be made from virtually any material. However, they are frustrating for children if they do not stay on effectively, so resources need to be chosen with care. Strong elastic is essential to ensure that full-face masks stay firmly in place.

MEETINGS

WHAT AND WHY? A group gathers together to plan, explore, present information, discuss ideas or resolve problems. It can be formal or informal, 'chaired' by teacher or child, and experienced in or out of 'role'. Meetings can also present further information, clarify what is happening in the drama, or create new tension. Some kind of signal, for example a special sign, sound, gesture or chair, is useful to call a meeting. It is essential that the children understand when a meeting is 'in role' and appreciate that roles must be sustained.

HOW? The teacher calls a meeting to tell all children in role as the 'townspeople' that a new king is coming from another kingdom. The teacher starts the meeting by saying, 'He is a dreadful man who might spoil our happy lives. What can we do?' The townspeople then discuss the situation.

RESOURCES Appropriate clothing, objects, symbols and so on, as required.

Scholastic
DRAMA
Workshop

MIME

WHAT AND WHY? The use of only physical movement, gesture and actions to express an idea, role or a dramatized scene. Mime may be accompanied by percussion, sound, nonsense vocabulary or music.

HOW? Children mime the scene when a group of explorers approach a dragon's den, while a child or the teacher narrates the events. The scene is then re-run in slow motion, so that all the actions are carefully considered.

RESOURCES Stimulus or support material, such as recorded music, percussion instruments, as appropriate.

MODELLING

WHAT AND WHY? The shaping and reshaping of the physical dimensions of a tableau or a drama scene, in pairs or in small groups. For example:
- in pairs – child A models child B into a tableau of a lost child at the seaside.
- in groups – child A models children B, C and D into a tableau of children caught in the act of creeping into a house, as they return home late.

HOW? The class work in pairs. One child in each pair models their partner into a tableau of someone who is going on holiday. The teacher then talks about this still image with the rest of the class.

RESOURCES None.

NARRATION

WHAT AND WHY?   An oral or written account of events. Narration has many uses: a teacher might provide narrative links in a drama; it can move a drama forward; it can create dramatic atmosphere. It can be used to focus on specific aspects, events, themes or issues, and the children or teacher may use narration either to tell a story or to provide structural links.

HOW?   Children act out the story of Hansel and Gretel while the teacher reads the narrative. The children take on the roles of the two characters and act out parts of the journey.

RESOURCES   As appropriate. Narrative passages can be prepared or improvised.

OVERHEARD CONVERSATIONS

WHAT AND WHY?   The children listen in to conversations between different sets of characters in the drama. Often the conversations are in different locations in the drama, for example a conversation in a police cell, and one in the family home of the person arrested.

HOW?   The children overhear a conversation in a pet shop about selling the animals cheaply because the shop is closing down. They then hear a family talking about pets not being cared for in the town. The children then explore how the conversations may be connected.

RESOURCES   None.

Scholastic
DRAMA
Workshop

PAPER LOCATION

WHAT AND WHY?   Strips of paper, material, card or wool mark an area on the floor to define the setting of a drama. Agree as a group exactly what the materials represent, for example the walls of a Saxon village, the huts, animals, plates, tables and so on. This is a convention which is ideal for focusing the whole class and building the context of a new topic.

HOW?   The children build a play area on the floor of their quiet corner. They decide on the range of play equipment, design the play area and 'mark' where an imaginary accident has taken place, for example where a person has been knocked over by a cyclist who has been cycling on the section of the pavement meant for pedestrians rather than in the cycle lane.

RESOURCES   Card, paper, wool, string, material, glue, 'bits and pieces'.

RE-ENACTMENT

WHAT AND WHY?   The process of revisiting a moment from a particular drama. It enables the class to examine a scene in more detail, in order to check facts, clarify detail and reflect on motives. The convention would normally operate in small groups and a scene could be re-enacted two or three times.

HOW?   A scene about road safety. A small child is knocked down by a bus at a pedestrian crossing and re-enactment helps to explore actions and their consequences.

RESOURCES   None.

ROLE ON THE WALL

WHAT AND WHY?   A simple drawing or a photograph of a character placed on the wall so that the children are aware of the 'character's' presence. The outline becomes the central focus for discussion about a particular role and is used to explore the feelings and motives of a character or as a starting point for the drama. Additional descriptive words may be included at any time to build a more comprehensive view. The best use of this convention is to lay a small child on some paper and draw around his or her outline in marker pen! On the inside of the body shape, write words which describe the character's feelings, emotions and actions; on the outside, write external influences, issues and motives. (These can be written by the teacher or by children.)

HOW?   A group draw a picture of the 'Big, Bad Wolf' from the story of The Three Little Pigs. They place words on the 'role' which describe the feelings and appearance of the wolf.

RESOURCES   Large pieces of paper and a broad felt-tipped pen for adding words or drawing a role.

ROLE REVERSAL

WHAT AND WHY?   At a key moment in the drama, selected by the teacher, children take on roles representing a different status, viewpoint or occupation. This is an effective convention for examining social interaction, opposing viewpoints, relationships and motives.

HOW?   In a drama about a toy shop all the children are in role as toys, talking about the big sale which is to start the next day. The teacher then reverses the roles and asks them to be parents and children attending the sale, talking about which toys they can afford and which ones they are thinking of buying.

RESOURCES   None.

Scholastic
DRAMA
Workshop

SMALL-GROUP PLAY-MAKING

WHAT AND WHY?
Small groups of children prepare a scene about a specific subject to express their feelings and understanding of the subject or situation. It is often used as an introduction or conclusion to a piece of dramatic exploration. Discussion is an important part of small-group play-making. It is important that the children are given time to talk during the process, to discuss plot and motivation. It is not always an easy convention for five- and six-year-olds. Problems can occur when children are constantly asked to show their plays, with no clear focus or reason, resulting in loss of interest, unproductive competition or an overemphasis on the humorous.

HOW?
The children create scenes relating to Christmas morning – opening presents, playing with toys or watching television, for example.

RESOURCES
As appropriate – none may be required.

SOUND COLLAGE

WHAT AND WHY?
Various sounds created by the children, either vocally or with instruments, performed to create the atmosphere of the place or environment where the drama is happening. The sounds can be voices, spoken words or singing put together, performed live or pre-recorded.

HOW?
Some children create noises and sounds to create a mysterious atmosphere for 'the wild woods', while others explore the woods through mime and movement, or create a still image or 'frozen picture' of the woods.

RESOURCES
Any sound-making objects, including voices, percussion instruments and so on. But feasibly, none!

TABLEAUX OR FREEZES

WHAT AND WHY? An image of a role, moment or an idea is represented, children using their bodies to create a likeness. Also known as a 'frozen moment', 'still picture', 'freeze-frame' or 'still image', this is a very easy convention to use. It encourages children to express their ideas and opinions simply, or to show a particular scene from a story or drama they have explored.

HOW? In a drama about a circus clown who cannot perform anymore, children create a tableau of the scene where all his tricks go wrong and everybody is mocking him.

RESOURCES None.

TEACHER-IN-ROLE

WHAT AND WHY? The teacher takes part in a drama. The participation can be high, medium or low status. Assuming a role, major or minor, helps the teacher to lead, build belief or tension, control, ask questions or extend ideas from 'inside' the drama. Used with whole-group drama, it is a more sophisticated dimension of hot-seating (see page 27). The children are also often in role in this convention and, for primary aged children, a teacher working alongside them in role can often help them to remain in role themselves.

HOW? The teacher takes the role of a senior citizen taking a pet to an animal welfare centre, with the children in role as vets. The drama explores how the pet can be cared for.

RESOURCES The teacher may use a representative prop or item of clothing to indicate being in or out of role, but this isn't always essential.

Scholastic
DRAMA
Workshop

TELEPHONE CONVERSATIONS

WHAT AND WHY?   The children overhear one or both sides of a telephone conversation between two characters 'in role'. This may be a one-way conversation, where the children hear one character talking in role to another character on the telephone, or a two-way conversation where both characters can be heard speaking on the telephone. This convention can be used to create interest and tension, provide information or news, explore motives and personal viewpoints, or create a new narrative.

HOW?   The children help the teacher-in-role as a toy-maker to make a toy. They receive a call from a customer asking the toy-maker to ensure the toy is a moving one. The toy-maker asks the children to help with the customer's request.

RESOURCES   Prop telephones can be used, but are not essential.

THOUGHT-TRACKING

WHAT AND WHY?   Individual children, in role, speak their inner thoughts. The teacher freezes the drama and taps a chosen character on the shoulder to indicate that they should speak their thoughts or feelings within the drama. Thought-tracking slows the action down by allowing it to pause, enables the children to reflect on events and establishes what the characters are thinking or feeling at a specific moment in the drama – which may or may not reflect what they have been saying out loud. This can be quite a difficult convention to do with younger children.

HOW?   The children all have similar roles, such as children on a visit to the zoo. They see an elephant that is hurt and the teacher asks them to describe what they are feeling as they look into the elephant's area in the zoo.

RESOURCES   None.

UNFINISHED MATERIALS

WHAT AND WHY? Incomplete information is used to initiate a drama. It may be an object, an article of clothing, an unfinished letter, a drawing or a newspaper cutting that gives a clue as to what the drama may be about. Often the children decide on the nature of the drama by interpreting the clues. The idea of continuing a story works well with young children.

HOW? The teacher tells the children part of a story about a little boy who gets lost and finds himself in a strange land. The children are told that the last pages of the story are missing and they then imagine and create the land, and the ending of the story.

RESOURCES Props, objects and so on, as determined by the drama. Ensure that any materials are chosen and gathered in advance of the lesson.

WHOLE-GROUP ROLE-PLAY

WHAT AND WHY? All of the class are in role at the same time, as required by a particular dramatic context, such as travellers on an aeroplane or inhabitants of a lost city. This convention can be the most demanding of all the conventions. If the focus is lost, the teacher must pause the developing drama and briefly discuss any difficulties before re-engaging participants.

HOW? The children assume roles of space explorers, climbing out of their spaceships to explore an imaginary, strange new planet. The teacher prepares and provides a complete narrative for the children to follow, describing the journey in the spaceship, the arrival on the planet and how the space explorers move around their new environment. The children respond to the narrative with mimed actions and appropriate dialogue.

RESOURCES As appropriate – none may be required.

Scholastic
DRAMA
Workshop

Chapter Four

DISCRETE ACTIVITIES

INTRODUCTION

This section of games and activities provides a simple but effective introduction to drama work. It is intended to give teachers the confidence to make that initial approach to try drama, with the help of clear instructions, specific guidance and support.

These short, one-off activities are established drama practices, with definable learning outcomes, through which children and teachers can begin to appreciate the aims and benefits of working with drama. They will help to:

- develop an atmosphere of trust and confidence between teacher and child
- release any tension arising from self-consciousness
- build confidence and self-esteem.
  Even the seemingly simple activities and games will help to:
- develop speaking and listening skills
- define drama 'rules'
- encourage appropriate responses, actions and reactions
- facilitate a supportive group atmosphere.

Discrete activities can be used alone or as part of a longer drama session, either by providing an introduction to the use of more complex conventions, or in order to establish a particular drama context or setting. In both of these respects, some of the games in this section may be found within the drama projects in Chapters Four to Ten of this book.

Individual games and activities can also be particularly successful if used as part of a whole-school approach to personal and social child development.

Learning outcomes can be implicit or explicit and will relate to at least one of the following elements:

- Personal and social development
- Communication skills
- Subject knowledge and understanding (drama or sometimes other curriculum subjects)
- Physical development
- Creative skills.

The sharing circle

As you can see from many of the activities included in this chapter, the use of a circle, whether the children sit, stand or kneel, is a common feature of drama teaching. It is a valuable way of promoting equal participation and a positive atmosphere. In an effective sharing circle:

- everyone has a chance to speak
- everyone is heard and listened to
- every contribution is respected
- the teacher asks questions that lead to discussion, rather than gives instructions
- the children feel able to volunteer.

The discrete activities in this chapter are arranged in order of difficulty. They progress from simple games and exercises to more complex individual activities. For ease of use and quick reference, the activities are organized using the following headings:

Learning outcomes or benefits: any skills, knowledge or development gained
Where? what space is required – that is, classroom, circle area or hall
What do you need? any resources or equipment
Process: what to do
Teacher guidance: support and advice
Variations or developments: any alternative methods or follow-on ideas.

Scholastic
DRAMA
Workshop

MUSICAL STATUES

LEARNING OUTCOMES OR BENEFITS:
- Physical development: a fun exercise which releases pent-up energy.
- Subject knowledge and understanding: (drama) an introduction to the concept of drama freezes.

WHERE?
School hall.

WHAT DO YOU NEED?
Recorded music and cassette player.

PROCESS:
1. Ask the children to stand in a space.
2. Explain to them that you will play some music which they must move to, but that when you pause or stop the music, they must stand very still and in complete silence.
3. Play the music and instruct the children to dance or move around the room to it. After a short while, pause or stop the music.
4. Eliminate anyone moving or making a sound when the music stops. Ask them to sit at the side.
5. Continue playing and pausing the music until you have a winner or winners.

TEACHER GUIDANCE:
- Use those children eliminated in the game to help you to spot others moving or making a noise when the music is paused.
- Advise the children to move carefully around the room – not only will this prevent injury, but it will be easier for them to stand absolutely still if they are not moving quickly!

VARIATIONS OR DEVELOPMENTS:
Use music with a 'theme' – animals, modes of transport and so on – and instruct the children to move accordingly. Ask all of the children to move together in a particular style – as elephants, as aeroplanes, as ballet dancers and so on.

UP, DOWN, FREEZE

LEARNING OUTCOMES OR BENEFITS:
- Communication skills: develops listening skills.
- Physical development: increases physical control.
- Personal and social development: builds concentration and quick responses.
- Subject knowledge and understanding: (drama) further development of the concept of 'drama freezes'.

WHERE?
School hall.

WHAT DO YOU NEED?
No specific equipment needed.

PROCESS:
1. Ask the children to stand in a space.
2. Inform them of the verbal commands you will be using and how they must respond.
3. Choose any or all of the verbal commands from the following:
   up = they must stand still with their arms raised in the air
   down = they must crouch down on the ground
   freeze = they should stand still and silent
   one leg = they must stand still on one leg
   heads = they should put their hands on their heads
   shoulders = they should put their hands on their shoulders
   turn = they must turn and face the opposite way, but not move
   go = they can continue moving.
4. Ask the children to walk around the room carefully, without bumping into each other, and to keep moving by walking into empty floor space.
5. Call out one of the commands for the children to respond to.
6. Eliminate the last children to respond to the command, or those not responding properly – that is, children not silent when responding to 'freeze', children wobbling when standing on 'one leg' and so on.
7. Ask the children to move around the room again, using the command 'go' and then, after a short while, call out another command for them to respond to.
8. Use commands any number of times and in any combinations.
9. Continue playing until you have a winner or winners.

TEACHER GUIDANCE:
- Use those children eliminated in the game to help you to spot others.
- Use as many or as few of the commands as meet the ability levels of the children in your class or group.

Scholastic
DRAMA
Workshop

3

DEAD LIONS

LEARNING OUTCOMES OR BENEFITS:
• Personal and social development: creates an atmosphere of calm and focus; establishes rules and the need to keep to them.

WHERE?
School hall.

WHAT DO YOU NEED?
No specific equipment needed.

PROCESS:
1. Choose two children to be 'lions'.
2. Ask all of the other children to lie down in a space on the hall floor. These children will be the 'dead lions'.
3. Instruct the two 'lions' to move among the other children and, without using physical contact, to try to make them move, laugh or make a sound.
4. Advise the 'dead lions' lying down not to move, giggle or even murmur in response to the 'lions'.
5. If any of the children lying down do move or make a sound, instruct them to join the other lions and try to make the remaining children respond.
6. Continue playing until the majority of children have become 'lions' and you have a winner or winners.

TEACHER GUIDANCE:
• Praise those children who manage to lie still and not respond to the 'lions' – this will encourage the other children not to 'fail'.

THE BEAR AND THE WOODCUTTERS

LEARNING OUTCOMES OR BENEFITS:
- Personal and social development: creates a dynamic of tension and anticipation; it is a game that everyone can play – there is no sense of failure.
- Subject knowledge and understanding: (drama) promotes a sense of 'role' as the children try not to respond to the 'bear'.

WHERE?
School hall.

WHAT DO YOU NEED?
No specific equipment needed.

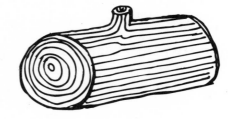

PROCESS:
1. Choose one child to be the 'bear'.
2. Tell the bear to stand with his or her back to the rest of the class.
3. Explain that the rest of the class are 'woodcutters' and that they should creep up on the bear as his or her back is turned.
4. Advise the bear that, after a short while, he or she should turn around and roar loudly at the woodcutters.
5. When the bear turns and roars at the woodcutters, they should quickly drop to the floor and lie still.
6. The bear should then move among the woodcutters and, without using physical contact, try to make them move or laugh.
7. Tell the woodcutters that they must try to keep very still and silent as the bear moves among them.
8. If any of the woodcutters laugh then they become another bear.
9. Continue playing the game until only a small group of woodcutters remain.

TEACHER GUIDANCE:
- In a large hall, restrict the area to enable the game to have a sense of closeness.
- Carefully select the first child to play the bear.
- Stay in close contact with the game, as it may be necessary to arbitrate.
- The game can be played as part of a weekly session. It is an excellent warm-up.

VARIATIONS OR DEVELOPMENTS:
Roles could be changed to suit a specific story, for example the 'bear' could become the 'wolf' and the 'woodcutters' changed to 'Little Red Riding Hood' or 'The Three Little Pigs'.

Scholastic
DRAMA
Workshop

PEOPLE TO PEOPLE

LEARNING OUTCOMES OR BENEFITS:

- Physical development: physical contact in a secure context; developing co-ordination and control; becoming aware of space.
- Personal and social development: co-operation and working together; mixing the groupings in the class to vary the social dynamic.

WHERE?

School hall.

WHAT DO YOU NEED?

No specific equipment needed.

PROCESS:

1. Ask the children to find a partner and stand in a space.
2. Call out instructions to the children which command them to link to their partner, using different parts of their bodies, for example hand to hand, knee to knee, elbow to ankle.
3. The pairs of children must follow each instruction, all at the same time, holding each of the positions given.
4. After repeating this process a few times, call out the command 'People to people!'
5. On this command, all of the children must form new pairs with a different partner.
6. Repeat the process of giving instructions and commanding the children to change partners as many times as you wish.

TEACHER GUIDANCE:

- This activity will work best if you give the directions for the whole of the first session, until the children are familiar with the idea and may then take over.
- If girls are working closely with boys, the activity will require careful and sensitive supervision.
- In a multicultural class there may be issues relating to contact, for example Muslim girls.

VARIATIONS OR DEVELOPMENTS:

One of the children, chosen carefully, could give the instructions.

FRUITBOWL

LEARNING OUTCOMES OR BENEFITS:
- Communication skills: develops speaking and listening skills.
- Personal and social development: promotes positive interaction and mixes the group; ensures no sense of failure; enables children to plan strategies for success.
- Physical development: promotes space awareness and develops co-ordination.

WHERE?
Large circle area or school hall.

WHAT DO YOU NEED?
A chair or cushion for each child.

PROCESS:
1. Sit the children on chairs or cushions in a circle.
2. In rotation, label the children with a 'fruit' name, for example apple, orange, banana, pear; apple, orange, banana, pear, until all the children are named.
3. Choose one child to stand in the middle of the circle and remove their chair or cushion, so that you now have one less seat than there are participants.
4. Instruct the child in the middle to call out one of the given fruit names.
5. Advise all of the other children sitting down that, if their fruit name is called out, they must swap seats across the circle.
6. Inform the child calling out the fruit name that he or she must also try to find a seat.
7. As there is one less seat than there are children, this process will result in a mad dash as everyone tries to find a seat! Tell the children that they cannot go back to their own seat in any one turn.
8. Each time a turn is played by a fruit name being called out, there will be one child left standing in the middle without a seat who must then call out the next fruit name for the process of swapping seats to begin again. (He or she can call two fruit names at the same time.)
9. Instruct the children that, if the child in the centre calls out 'fruitbowl!' then everyone in the circle must swap seats.

TEACHER GUIDANCE:
- Ensure that there are sufficient chairs/cushions for each child at the start of the game.
- Emphasize the need for light, speedy movements and warn against any physical contact or pushing.
- Watch carefully for very clever cheats who 'drift' from the centre to stand near to the chair of a person with the fruit name they are about to call – there are many who will do this!
- Advise those children left in the centre to speak loudly and clearly.

Scholastic
DRAMA
Workshop

NAME TRAIN

LEARNING OUTCOMES OR BENEFITS:
- Personal and social development: positive whole-class activity involving physical contact; taking turns and co-operating; understanding and abiding by a set of rules; learning names of other children in the class.
- Communication skills: develops listening skills.

WHERE?
Large circle area or school hall.

WHAT DO YOU NEED?
No specific equipment needed.

PROCESS:
1. Ask all of the children to sit in a circle.
2. Nominate one child to be the 'train engine'.
3. Ask the train engine to move around the inside of the circle, listening for you to call out the name of a station.
4. Advise the child who is the train engine that, when they hear you name a station (for example, Euston) they are to stop moving immediately and call out the name of the child they are standing in front of.
5. If they are named correctly, that child must then link onto the back of the train engine, by holding on around their waist.
6. The train must then continue moving around the circle until you call out another station name, when the train engine must stop, call out the name of the child who it is standing in front of, link up another 'carriage' and then continue moving.
7. Turn your back as the train engine is moving, so that you cannot see where the child is when you call out the station name.
8. Continue the process until all, or the majority of children, have become one large train moving around the circle.

TEACHER GUIDANCE:
- This activity will need careful co-ordination if played in a confined space.
- Try to ensure that every child has a turn at either being the train engine, or one of the train carriages. When the circle is depleted, you will still have your back to the children, but you will need to check that the engine is near to a child when you call out the station name.
- Choose your first 'train engine' carefully.
- You can use the same name or a variety of different station names.

VARIATIONS OR DEVELOPMENTS:
Ask one of the children to call out the station name. Add a rhythm or a simple song which can be created or sung as the train moves around.

LOOK DOWN, LOOK UP

LEARNING OUTCOMES OR BENEFITS:
- Personal and social development: requires total concentration and silence; insists on honesty and fair play.
- Communication skills: excellent for promoting eye contact.

WHERE?
Large circle area or school hall.

WHAT DO YOU NEED?
No specific equipment required.

PROCESS:
1. Ask the children to stand in a circle.
2. Inform them that when you instruct them to 'Look down', they are to look directly at the floor.
3. Advise them that then, when they hear your command to 'Look up', they are to make direct eye contact with another person standing in the circle.
4. Insist that they understand that 'looking up' does not mean staring at the ceiling!
5. Inform the children that when they look up, if the person they are looking at is also looking at them, then they are both out and must sit down.
6. Tell the children that they must make direct and instant eye contact with another person standing in the circle when instructed to do so, and that they must not pretend to be looking at someone else should they discover that that person is also looking at them!
7. Ensure that all of the children understand the rules and accept that cheats will not be tolerated, and then give the command for them to 'Look down'.
8. Follow this, after a short beat pause, with the command for the children to 'Look up'.
9. Any pairs looking at each other must sit down and take no further part in the game.
10. Continue giving the command to 'Look down, look up' until you have a winner or winners.
11. Repeat as required!

TEACHER GUIDANCE:
- Children will use various methods to cheat at this game – exclude any cheats from the game instantly!
- As the numbers still playing dwindle, ask the remaining children to take a small step inwards to reduce the circle size.
- Keep those who are 'out' occupied by asking them to help you to watch the others for cheats.
- Walk around the outside of the circle continuously as you give the commands; it makes the children very aware of your presence!
- Insist on the silence of those who are 'out'.

Scholastic
DRAMA
Workshop

9

TANGLE

LEARNING OUTCOMES OR BENEFITS:
- Personal and social development: encourages the class to work together positively; introduces physical contact.
- Physical development: strengthens self-discipline and control.

WHERE?
School hall.

WHAT DO YOU NEED?
No specific equipment needed.

PROCESS:

1. Nominate two children to be the 'untanglers' and ask them to leave the room (if practical) or to turn their backs on the rest of the class.
2. Ask the remaining children to hold hands in a circle and then instruct them to create an enormous 'tangle' by moving under and over one another's arms.
3. Advise the children creating the tangle that they must not break the link by releasing hands.
4. Once the tangle has been completed, reintroduce the 'untanglers' to see if they can undo the tangle by physically reversing the actions of the rest of the class and returning them to a complete circle, without any child letting go of their neighbours' hands!
5. Allow the 'untanglers' a short period of time to achieve this aim.
6. Regardless of whether the 'untanglers' manage to undo the tangle or not, release the circle, nominate two new 'untanglers' and repeat the process.

TEACHER GUIDANCE:
- Ensure that the rules are clear and fully understood before starting this exercise.
- You must make yourself aware of: children getting hurt, children behaving in a manner which could result in injury and children cheating by dropping and then re-forming hands.
- This will not be a quiet activity!

VARIATIONS OR DEVELOPMENTS:
After a few attempts, make the task more difficult by asking the children to 'tangle' in silence!

WINK MURDER

LEARNING OUTCOMES OR BENEFITS:
- Communication skills: provides an introduction to non-verbal communication.
- Personal and social development: builds whole-group approach; creates tension and focus.
- Creative skills/subject knowledge and understanding: (drama) introduces a sense of role and character response.

WHERE?
Large circle area or school hall.

WHAT DO YOU NEED?
No specific equipment needed.

PROCESS:
1. Ask the children to sit in a circle, on chairs or on the floor.
2. Choose one child to be the 'detective' and either ask him or her to leave the room, or to turn around.
3. Instruct the remaining children to close their eyes and bow their heads, so as not to see.
4. Walk around the outside of the circle and tap one of the children on the back; this child has now become the 'murderer'. The murderer must not be revealed to the other players.
5. Explain that the murderer is going to 'murder' children sitting in the circle by winking silently at them.
6. Reintroduce the detective, asking him or her to stand in the centre of the circle and to watch the children carefully.
7. Instruct the murderer to go ahead and advise those children who are 'wink murdered' to die horribly and dramatically!
8. Tell the detective to try and guess who the murderer is. Allow him or her three guesses.
9. Advise all of the children to try not to reveal who the murderer is.
10. If the detective doesn't guess correctly in three goes, reveal the murderer then by asking him or her to stand up.
11. Choose a new detective and murderer and begin the game again.

TEACHER GUIDANCE:
- Those children who cannot wink can blink both eyes instead.
- Try to ensure that you balance the sexes of the children chosen.
- Insist on total silence – only broken by ear-piercing screams!
- Please be advised that children will happily play this game for an inordinately long period of time!

VARIATIONS OR DEVELOPMENTS:
Choose two murderers to make the game more interesting! Use the game as an introduction to role-playing detectives, devising murder mysteries or creative writing.

MOVE TO THE BEAT

LEARNING OUTCOMES OR BENEFITS:
- Physical development controlled movement.
- Creative skills: using imaginative responses.
- Subject knowledge and understanding: (music) can be used as an introduction to counting musical beats.

WHERE?
School hall.

WHAT DO YOU NEED?
Recorded music or instruments (optional).

PROCESS:
1. Ask the children to find a space and to curl up in a tight ball, as small as they possibly can, on the floor.
2. Instruct them to gradually uncurl, get up and stretch until their arms, hands and fingertips are completely extended upwards and they are standing on tiptoes.
3. Reverse the process, asking the children to move slowly from this extended position into a tight ball again.
4. Repeat both movement sequences.
5. Finally, ask the children to relax their bodies by lying flat out on the floor.

TEACHER GUIDANCE:
- The emphasis should be on controlling movements, not on seeing who can move the fastest.
- Insist that the exercise be performed in silence, to create a calm focus.

VARIATIONS OR DEVELOPMENTS:
Use slow, soothing music to encourage fluidity of movement. Or use a drum or tambourine and instruct the children to time each individual move, as they uncurl and curl, to each beat. Limit the number of beats (and moves) so that in, for example, 20 beats they must have moved from the curled-up position to the extended position. Then reduce or extend the number of beats (and moves).

12

WALKABOUT (1)

LEARNING OUTCOMES OR BENEFITS:
- Physical development: develops controlled movement and spatial awareness.
- Personal and social development: encourages co-operation and consideration for others.
- Creative skills: develops spontaneous thought and imaginative responses.
- Communication skills: highlights the need to listen carefully to instructions.

WHERE?
School hall.

WHAT DO YOU NEED?
No specific equipment needed.

PROCESS:
1. Ask the children to walk around the room as naturally as possible, looking for empty floor space to move into, without touching or bumping into anyone.
2. After a while, ask them to continue moving, but walking as far away from everyone else as possible.
3. Then instruct them to walk as close as they can to everyone else, still without touching or bumping into anyone.
4. Finally, ask them to walk about naturally again and advise them that, on your command of 'Change!' they must walk in a different direction, still without touching or bumping into anyone else.
5. Allow the children to continue walking around the room, giving the 'Change!' command to vary their movements as often as required.

TEACHER GUIDANCE:
- Emphasize the rules of behaviour prior to starting to ensure safety.
- Remove any children from the exercise who are being silly and who may be a danger to others.
- Praise those children who respond quickly and accurately to your commands.

VARIATIONS OR DEVELOPMENTS:
Instruct the children to walk as slowly as possible. Similarly, instruct them to walk as quickly as possible, without actually running; to walk backwards; to skip; to hop; to walk around with their eyes closed (ensure careful supervision for this variation). Create a pattern of several different methods of movement, moving from one to another by use of the 'Change!' command.

Scholastic
DRAMA
Workshop

WALKABOUT (2)

LEARNING OUTCOMES OR BENEFITS:
- Physical development: develops controlled movement and spatial awareness.
- Personal and social development: encourages co-operation and consideration for others; creates no sense of failure.
- Creative skills: develops spontaneous thought and imaginative responses.
- Communication skills: develops listening skills.

WHERE?
School hall.

WHAT DO YOU NEED?
Recorded music or instruments (optional).

PROCESS:
1. Ask the children to move carefully around the room, without bumping into or touching each other, travelling in any way that they wish.
2. Advise them that, on your command of 'Change!', they must alter their mode of movement – for example, if they began by walking, they must now hop, skip, crawl and so on.
3. Tell the children that they cannot use the same mode of movement twice.
4. Instruct them to continue moving around the room, and use the 'Change!' command a number of times to encourage the children to try a variety of different movement methods.

TEACHER GUIDANCE:
- Ensure that you praise original methods of movement.
- Gradually decrease the amount of time between each 'Change!' command, in order to encourage swift responses.

VARIATIONS OR DEVELOPMENTS:
Use recorded music or an instrument to instigate the changes instead of a verbal command – when the music stops or the instrument is sounded, the children must use a different movement style.

Instruct the children that they must move around without using their feet, for example sliding on their tummies, shuffling on their bottoms, walking on their knees, and so on.

14

WALKABOUT (3)

LEARNING OUTCOMES OR BENEFITS:
- Physical development: develops controlled movement and spatial awareness.
- Subject knowledge and understanding: (drama) introduces the concept of mime; (science) excellent introduction to animal topics; (music) introduces basic musical interpretation.
- Creative skills: stimulates the use of imaginative movement; provides a basis for presentation or performance.
- Personal and social development: builds self-confidence within a comfortable group context.

WHERE?
School hall.

WHAT DO YOU NEED?
Recorded music or instruments (optional).

PROCESS:
1. Sit the children in a circle, and discuss the way that different animals move.
2. Ask the children to stand in a space in the hall and to think of an animal.
3. Instruct the children that, on your command of 'Go!', they are to move around the room as if they were their chosen animal.
4. Advise them that they are to move carefully, without bumping into each other.
5. Praise their efforts.
6. After a while, give the command 'Stop!'
7. Now ask the children to think of another animal, and repeat the process.
8. Command them to 'stop!' again.
9. Ask all the children with the same choice of animal to move together, while the others sit and observe.
10. Repeat this process as many times as there are multiple choices of animals.
11. Sit the children in a circle again and discuss their different movements, particularly emphasizing how realistic they were.

TEACHER GUIDANCE:
- Ensure that all efforts are praised.
- If your children lack confidence, ignore the 'performance' and 'audience' stages until you feel they are ready.

VARIATIONS OR DEVELOPMENTS:
Use instruments or recorded music to represent the animals and ask the children to respond with their animal movements. Use the same process to ask the children to move around the room as different types of people, for example a police officer, a ballet dancer, an old person, a tightrope walker, someone carrying a heavy parcel, a farmer, a clown and so on.

Scholastic
DRAMA
Workshop

15

THE SPY GAME

LEARNING OUTCOMES OR BENEFITS:
- Personal and social education: requires control and concentration; asks children to complete two tasks simultaneously.
- Physical development: develops confidence in movement and spatial awareness.
- Creative skills: creates an imaginative whole-class response.

WHERE?
School hall.

WHAT DO YOU NEED?
No specific equipment needed.

PROCESS:
1. Ask the children to stand on their own in a space.
2. Instruct them to mentally select someone in the group they would like to follow.
3. Ask the children to move around the room, following their chosen person, without letting the person know.
4. Each child should now be surreptitiously following someone, while also trying to work out who is following them.
5. After a suitable time, stop the game to allow each child to disclose which person they have been following.
6. Discuss with the children how difficult it was to remain inconspicuous when following their chosen person, while also trying to discover who was following them.

TEACHER GUIDANCE:
- Insist on silence when the game is underway.
- Encourage the children to go and tell each other who they have been following.
- Play the game through two or three times and encourage the children to keep changing the person they are following.
- Be aware that some children may not be chosen to be followed and prepare for this occurring.

ROCKS IN THE SEA

LEARNING OUTCOMES OR BENEFITS:
- Creative skills: creative and controlled use of the imagination.
- Personal and social development: creates self-discipline, co-operation, trust and control; requires complete concentration and focus.
- Communication skills: develops listening skills.

WHERE?
School hall.

WHAT DO YOU NEED?
Blindfolds (optional).

PROCESS:
1. Nominate half of the class to be 'rocks' and ask them to sit in spaces all over the hall.
2. Inform the remaining children that they are 'ships'.
3. Tell the 'ships' that they are to close their eyes and move around the hall without hitting or bumping into the 'rocks'.
4. Instruct the 'rocks' to make the noise of waves crashing against the shore to help the 'ships' to safety by avoiding crashing into them.
5. Ask the 'ships' to move slowly and cautiously around the room with their eyes closed, listening carefully for the 'rocks' to avoid crashing into any of them.
6. After a while, swap the 'rocks' and the 'ships' over and repeat the process.
7. Allow the exercise to run for a couple of turns and then gather the children together to discuss how difficult it was.

TEACHER GUIDANCE:
- Depending upon the size and shape of the space, it is probably best to ask the 'ships' to make their way together – that is, from one wall of the room to another.
- If the children find it difficult to close their eyes for a sustained period, it may be better to choose one or two confident volunteers at a time as 'ships' and to use a blindfold on each of them.
- Emphasize the need for the 'ships' to move slowly and carefully.

VARIATIONS OR DEVELOPMENTS:
Ask the 'ships' to close their eyes, and then move the 'rocks' around, so that the 'ships' are unable to memorize the position of the 'rocks'.

Scholastic
DRAMA
Workshop

LEADING FRIENDS

LEARNING OUTCOMES OR BENEFITS:
- Creative skills: develops creative responses.
- Physical development: using the imagination in movement; develops spatial awareness.
- Personal and social development: builds co-operation and trust.
- Communication skills: develops listening skills.

WHERE?
School hall.

WHAT DO YOU NEED?
Blindfolds (optional).

PROCESS:
1. Ask the children to find a partner.
2. Instruct them that one partner is to close his or her eyes and will be guided around the room by the other child.
3. Inform the children that initially the guidance will be purely physical and silent, for example a touch on the shoulder or hand.
4. Ask the children to decide who will be led and who will be the leader. Tell the children being led to close their eyes.
5. Instruct the leaders to guide their partners around the room, ensuring that they are safe at all times.
6. Allow this process to continue for a few moments and then ask the children to swap over, so that leaders now become those who are led.
7. Allow the activity to continue for a short while.
8. Inform the leaders that they are now to use spoken instructions (without any physical contact) to guide their partners safely around the room, avoiding other children. (For example, 'Stop! Turn. Move forwards. Move backwards.')
9. Emphasize the need for children to listen carefully to their partner's voice only.
10. Allow this process to continue for a few moments and then ask the children to swap over, as before.
11. Stop the activity and discuss with the children how difficult it was to concentrate on their partners and to be led by another person.

TEACHER GUIDANCE:
- This is an activity which demands a quiet, concentrated approach.
- Emphasize the need for careful movement and consideration at all times between partners.

VARIATIONS OR DEVELOPMENTS:
If the children find the exercise difficult, the child being led can open his or her eyes occasionally. If necessary, use blindfolds and two confident children at a time to demonstrate this activity and gradually build to whole-group involvement.

CATCH MY NAME

LEARNING OUTCOMES OR BENEFITS:
- Personal and social development: involves whole-group concentration and focus; builds self-discipline and teaches children to take turns; increases self-confidence.
- Communication skills: develops eye contact and non-verbal communication; enables children to learn names of classmates.
- Physical development: provides physical action in a secure setting; aids development of fine motor skills.

WHERE?
Classroom, circle area or school hall.

WHAT DO YOU NEED?
A beanbag or very soft ball.

PROCESS:
1. Ask the children to sit in a circle or in their classroom places.
2. Nominate one child to start and instruct him or her to throw the beanbag to another, calling out the name of the intended receiver as the beanbag is thrown.
3. Instruct the second child to catch the beanbag, then to call out the name of a third child and throw the beanbag again.
4. Allow this process of throwing and catching to continue, with no specific pattern, until every child has had at least one turn in either throwing or catching the beanbag.
5. Gradually advise the children to increase the pace for throwing and catching the beanbag.

TEACHER GUIDANCE:
- If particular children are initially shy, the teacher should not allow others to pressure them to join in until they are ready.
- If the children are sitting in a circle, it should be close and tight.
- Encourage the children to make a concerted effort to throw and catch the beanbag accurately.

VARIATIONS OR DEVELOPMENTS:
Gradually introduce additional beanbags, so that two, or even three, are in the process of being caught and thrown at the same time.

Instruct the children to make silent eye contact with someone else sitting in the circle, throw the beanbag to them without calling their name, and the person who catches it then calls out the name of the thrower. When the children become proficient at this process, introduce additional beanbags, so that the throwing and catching response requires much greater concentration levels.

Nominate one child to sit on a chair in the middle of the circle. Instruct him or her to call out the name of one of the other children and throw the beanbag to them. Tell the receiver to then throw it back, calling out the name of the person sitting in the middle. Continue with this process for a few turns and then change the person sitting in the middle.

Scholastic
DRAMA
Workshop

ANIMAL FAMILIES

LEARNING OUTCOMES OR BENEFITS:
- Personal and social development: builds confidence through whole-group interaction; develops concentration.
- Communication skills: introduces verbal communication skills; develops listening skills.
- Subject knowledge and understanding: (science) animal categories can be linked to curriculum topics; (maths) understanding and making number groups.

WHERE?
Large classroom or school hall.

WHAT DO YOU NEED?
Animal pictures or names on paper (at least four of each animal).

PROCESS:
1. Give each child the name or a picture of an animal.
2. Ensure that there are at least four children for each animal.
3. Ask the children to mix up and move around, making appropriate sounds for their animal, for example, for a cow 'Moo…'
4. Explain that they have to listen and meet up with other animals the same as themselves.

TEACHER GUIDANCE:
- Emphasize the importance of making the sounds continuously and of listening attentively.

VARIATIONS OR DEVELOPMENTS:
Ask the children to close their eyes to highlight the importance of listening for their animal sounds. Apply the same process to modes of transport, seaside sounds – in fact anything topical which can be used as a basis for 'sound' groupings.

LONDON'S BURNING

LEARNING OUTCOMES OR BENEFITS:
- Communication skills: responding to verbal instructions; develops speaking and listening skills.
- Personal and social development: planning strategies for success; develops confidence through whole-group focus.

WHERE?
Classroom or school hall.

WHAT DO YOU NEED?
A suitable object to hide.

PROCESS:
1. Show all of the children the object which you intend to hide.
2. Nominate two children to be the 'finders' and ask them to either leave the room or hide themselves, so that they cannot see what you are doing.
3. Once the 'finders' are absent, hide your chosen object somewhere in the room while the remaining children observe.
4. Ask the two 'finders' to re-enter and instruct them that they have to find the hidden object.
5. Ask the rest of the class to sing the song 'London's burning' and instruct them to sing more loudly if the 'finders' move closer to where the object is, and more quietly if they move further away.
6. Continue until the object is found. Choose two new 'finders' and repeat the process.

TEACHER GUIDANCE:
- Ensure that the remaining children are constructive in their singing and provide assistance to the 'finders'.
- Recap the rules for the remaining children prior to them singing and have a trial run of increasing and decreasing the volume.
- Ensure that the remaining children do not use the exercise as an excuse to humiliate the 'finders'.

Scholastic
DRAMA
Workshop

CHINESE WHISPERS

LEARNING OUTCOMES OR BENEFITS:
- Communication skills: develops speaking and listening skills; explores the concept of processing information.
- Personal and social development: creates a positive and productive tension; encourages whole-group verbal interaction.

WHERE?
Circle area or school hall.

WHAT DO YOU NEED?
No specific equipment needed.

PROCESS:
1. Sit in a circle with the children. Ensure that each child is close to their neighbour.
2. Tell them that a message is going to be passed around the circle, with each child whispering it to the child on their left.
3. Inform the children that they must pass on exactly what they hear from their neighbour, and that the message cannot be repeated once it has been whispered.
4. Decide on a short message or sentence and whisper it to the child on your left.
5. Instruct this child to then whisper exactly what he or she heard to the child on their left.
6. Continue to pass the message around the whole class in this manner.
7. Ask the final child to speak out loud the message he or she received.
8. Reveal your original message and see how much it has changed as it travelled around the circle.
9. Discuss with the children why they think the message became so distorted.

TEACHER GUIDANCE:
- Be very careful in your choice of original message; some distortions can result in very rude final messages!
- Ensure that the rules are very clear and understood prior to starting and that children know that they cannot ask for the message to be repeated.

VARIATIONS OR DEVELOPMENTS:
Once the children are familiar with this exercise, nominate one of them to send the original message, but choose this child carefully.

WHAT'S MISSING?

LEARNING OUTCOMES OR BENEFITS:
- Personal and social development: develops observation skills and use of memory.
- Communication skills: encourages honest and focused responses.

WHERE?
Circle area or school hall.

WHAT DO YOU NEED?
A selection of eight to twelve easily recognizable objects.

PROCESS:
1. Gather together your objects and place them close at hand.
2. Sit in a circle with the children.
3. Place your chosen objects on the floor in the middle of the circle.
4. Inform the children that they have 15 seconds to memorize the objects and allow them that time.
5. Ask the children to close their eyes or turn their backs on the objects.
6. Remove one of the objects and secrete it where it cannot be seen by the children.
7. Ask the children to open their eyes, or to turn around again, and to say which object has been removed.
8. When the children have revealed the correct answer, replace the object, move all of the objects around and repeat the process.

TEACHER GUIDANCE:
- Encourage children to respond by putting their hands up if they want to say which object has been removed.
- Choose your objects carefully and ensure that they are all easily recognizable to the children.

VARIATIONS OR DEVELOPMENTS:
As the children become more proficient at this exercise, increase the number of objects, or introduce objects which are not familiar to them.

23

SOUND ORCHESTRA

LEARNING OUTCOMES OR BENEFITS:
- Communication skills: develops verbal skills; improves listening skills; encourages appropriate responses.
- Personal and social development: concentrated whole-group work; builds confidence through individual participation.
- Subject knowledge and understanding: (music) provides an introduction to musical expression.

WHERE?
Classroom, circle area or school hall.

WHAT DO YOU NEED?
No specific equipment needed.

PROCESS:
1. Ask the children to sit in a circle or in their classroom places.
2. Inform them that you are going to make a sound very softly and then ask them to repeat the sound at an increased volume level.
3. Make your initial sound (for example, a faint sound of the wind whistling) and then encourage the children to copy it at a louder volume.
4. Inform the children that you are now going to 'conduct' them as they make the sound. Tell them that they must all keep to the same volume level.
5. Show the children hand signals which they must respond to: (a) to increase the volume of the sound (for example, raising hands, with arms outstretched and palms upward), (b) to decrease the volume of the sound (for example, lowering hands, arms outstretched and palms downwards), and (c) to stop making any sound (for example, making a 'slicing', cross-over movement with arms outstretched and palms downwards).
6. Advise all the children that they must respond instantly to your hand signals.
7. Using the same or a different sound, 'conduct' the children, using the appropriate hand signals to indicate when they should increase and decrease the volume level or stop completely.
8. Choose another sound and repeat the process.

TEACHER GUIDANCE:
- Choose any volunteers carefully (see below).
- Gradually empower children with more control of this exercise, so that it is not always the teacher who makes the initial sound and performs the hand signals.

VARIATIONS OR DEVELOPMENTS:
Allow a child to 'conduct' the class or appoint individual conductors for small groups. Use recognizable words, or words from other languages, instead of abstract sounds. Orchestrate the recognizable words into full sentences, with small groups each 'performing' a different word or phrase within the sentence.

PASS IT ON!

LEARNING OUTCOMES OR BENEFITS:
- Personal and social development: whole-group concentrated activity; builds confidence through individual participation.
- Creative skills: develops creative expression.
- Subject knowledge and understanding: (drama) introduces the concept of mime.

WHERE?
Circle corner or school hall.

WHAT DO YOU NEED?
No specific equipment needed.

PROCESS:
1. Sit in a circle with the children.
2. Inform them that you are going to make a facial expression and that they must all pass this 'face' on around the circle and back to you.
3. Advise them that the facial expression must remain the same all the way around.
4. Make a particular facial expression, for example a smile, a frown or a funny face, and 'pass it on' to the child sitting on your left, instructing them to 'pass it on' to their neighbour.
5. Continue passing the facial expression around the circle until it is finally passed back to you, still in its original form.
6. Repeat the process, passing on different expressions.

TEACHER GUIDANCE:
- Insist on the exercise being completed as quietly as possible, preferably in complete silence!
- Choose the child to lead very carefully (see below).
- Praise any good efforts, but not to the detriment of those who may be trying hard.

VARIATIONS OR DEVELOPMENTS:
Other ideas to 'pass on' around the circle include a gesture, a hand signal, a noise, a movement sequence or a simple mime. (Ask the children to offer any other suggestions.)

Choose one of the children to 'pass something on' around the circle. Or send two different facial expressions (perhaps ones that are opposite to each other) in two different directions around the circle at the same time, one going clockwise, the other anticlockwise.

Use this process to add 'actions' to a story. For example, read the story of Goldilocks and the Three Bears and pause to express how she was feeling, what the bears felt, her actions and so on.

PASS THE SQUEEZE

LEARNING OUTCOMES OR BENEFITS:
- Personal and social development: compels the group to work together; focuses concentration and co-operation.
- Physical development: a non-threatening way of developing physical contact.
- Communication skills: provides an alternative form of non-verbal communication.

WHERE?
Circle area or school hall.

WHAT DO YOU NEED?
No specific equipment needed.

PROCESS:
1. Stand or sit with the children in a circle and instruct everyone to join hands.
2. Inform the children that you are going to pass a 'squeeze' around the circle from hand to hand and that, when they feel their hand squeezed, they should then pass it on by squeezing their neighbour's hand.
3. Ask the children to be as quiet as possible while passing the squeeze around.
4. Squeeze the hand of the child holding your right hand.
5. Watch and wait for the squeeze to make its journey around the circle and announce when it arrives back to you.
6. Repeat the process, passing the squeeze in the opposite direction.

TEACHER GUIDANCE:
- This is an effective activity for creating a quiet focus.
- Children may find it difficult at first, so repetition is advised prior to development.
- Watch carefully for one or two individuals who may try to cheat the system!

VARIATIONS OR DEVELOPMENTS:
Nominate a child to begin and end the squeeze. Or pass two squeezes along at the same time, in different directions.

Instruct the children to pass the squeeze with their eyes closed and see what happens! Time how long it takes to pass the squeeze (eyes open or eyes closed) around the circle and then try to beat it!

Choose two children to go into the centre of the circle and try to 'catch' the squeeze – that is, to spot where it is in the circle. Ask them to close their eyes while the 'starter' is nominated. Explain that when you say 'The game starts now!' they can open their eyes to try to 'catch' the squeeze.

WHO'S LEADING THE MOVEMENT?

LEARNING OUTCOMES OR BENEFITS:
- Personal and social development: creates a whole-group focus; builds concentration; develops instinctive and appropriate reactions to others.
- Communication skills: develops use of eye contact; builds non-verbal communication skills.

WHERE?
Classroom, circle area or school hall.

WHAT DO YOU NEED?
No specific equipment needed.

PROCESS:
1. Ask the children to stand or sit in a circle.
2. Select one child to leave the room or turn away from the rest of the class – he or she is the 'observer'.
3. Without the first child seeing, nominate a second child to lead the rest of the circle in a series of simple, continuous movements – tapping a foot, nodding heads, waving arms and so on – he or she is the 'movement leader'.
4. Instruct all of the circle to copy the movement leader.
5. Reintroduce the observer, asking him or her to stand in the centre of the circle.
6. Inform the movement leader that he or she must continue leading the rest of the children in a series of movement patterns, while the observer watches.
7. Advise the children copying the movement leader that they must continue to imitate the movements, without revealing who the leader is.
8. The movement leader can change the movements as many times as he or she wishes.
9. Allow the observer two or three guesses to discover who is leading the movements.

TEACHER GUIDANCE:
- Select the children to lead and guess very carefully. Some children will find either role rather daunting.

VARIATIONS OR DEVELOPMENTS:
Nominate two or more children to guess. (This would help less confident children to feel more secure.)

Ask the movement leader to perform simple mimes instead, for example combing their hair, cleaning their teeth, making a pancake and so on.

Scholastic
DRAMA
Workshop

FREEZE IN ROLE

LEARNING OUTCOMES OR BENEFITS:
- Personal and social development: builds concentration.
- Communication skills: develops listening skills.
- Subject knowledge and understanding: (drama) generates awareness of drama freezes; builds ability to create roles.
- Physical development: develops physical control and spatial awareness.
- Creative skills: prompts the use of spontaneous imaginative response.

WHERE?
School hall.

WHAT DO YOU NEED?
A whistle (optional).

PROCESS:
1. Ask the children to walk carefully around the room, looking for empty floor space to move into.
2. Inform the children that, when you blow your whistle or clap your hands, they are to listen carefully.
3. Tell the children that you will then shout out the name of a job, occupation or role and they are to 'freeze' (standing still and silent) in the position of someone in that particular role.
4. After a short while, blow a whistle or clap your hands and then call out the name of a job, occupation or role, for example hairdresser, firefighter, pop star, doctor and so on.
5. The children must then immediately freeze as instructed.
6. Ask the children to 'hold' their freezes – being as still and silent as possible – for a few seconds. Praise their efforts.
7. Then instruct the children to move around the room again.
8. After another short period of moving, give your signal again and call out a new role for them to freeze in.

TEACHER GUIDANCE:
- Some children will panic at the spontaneous aspect of this exercise and will (a) either not be able to think of anything or (b) copy what everyone else is doing. This is perfectly understandable and acceptable.
- Give children the time and encouragement to build their confidence and they will eventually be able to respond immediately.
- Try to respond positively to every child's efforts, whether it is their ability to freeze or the accurate portrayal of the role.

VARIATIONS OR DEVELOPMENTS:
Use this process for any topics – animals, school life, things found at the seaside, and so on.

COPY CAT

LEARNING OUTCOMES OR BENEFITS:
- Physical development: develops spatial awareness and physical control.
- Personal and social development: encourages co-operation; builds concentration.
- Communication skills: develops non-verbal communication skills.

WHERE?
School hall.

WHAT DO YOU NEED?
Recorded music (optional).

PROCESS:
1. Ask the children to find a partner, and instruct them to kneel on the floor, facing their partners.
2. Inform them that, on your command of 'Start', they are to move together and rise slowly from their kneeling positions until they are both standing upright with their arms and fingers stretching upwards.
3. Advise the children that their movements should be synchronized and partners should make every effort to 'grow' together.
4. When the children understand what is expected of them, give the 'Start' command.
5. When all of the pairs have reached the upright position, you should then command them to 'Freeze', asking them to all pause, remaining still and silent.
6. Inform the children that, on your repeat command of 'Start', they must reverse the process of synchronized movements until both partners are back to the initial kneeling position again.
7. When the children understand what is expected of them, give the repeat command of 'Start'.
8. Advise the children that these synchronized movements should be completed with no verbal communication.
9. Repeat the 'growing' and 'shrinking' movement process as required.

TEACHER GUIDANCE:
- With a noisy group, introduce the notion of silent work gradually.
- Repeat the initial, simple process as many times as required before moving on to a more complex approach.
- The aim is to ensure that all children eventually move instinctively at the same pace as their partners.
- Ask the children to change partners regularly, in order that they learn to work with a variety of different people.

VARIATIONS OR DEVELOPMENTS:
Use suitable recorded music to control the speed of the movements. Vary the moves and the starting or finishing positions.

Scholastic
DRAMA
Workshop

MIRRORS

LEARNING OUTCOMES OR BENEFITS:
- Personal and social development: develops co-operation and focuses concentration; encourages children to respond to each other.
- Communication skills: compels children to make eye contact.
- Physical development: develops a sense of co-ordination; increases the ability to perform controlled movements.
- Creative skills: develops the ability to plan and execute an imaginative sequence.

WHERE?
School hall.

WHAT DO YOU NEED?
No specific equipment needed.

PROCESS:
1. Ask the children to find a partner and stand in a space, facing their partner.
2. Tell the children to number themselves, either 1 or 2, and inform them that number 1's represent a mirror, while number 2's are 'looking into' the mirror.
3. Advise the children that 'mirrors' must copy exactly any actions that their partners perform.
4. Provide guidance for the children regarding the synchronization of arm and leg movements: mirrors should reflect movements exactly, therefore if the person looking into the mirror raises their right leg, the mirror would raise its left leg.
5. Ask the children to prepare and execute a simple mirrored mime sequence of someone getting washed, cleaning their teeth and combing their hair in the morning.
6. Advise the children to plan and co-ordinate their movements to the finest detail.
7. Allow a short period of time for the children to attempt this process, providing assistance where needed.

TEACHER GUIDANCE:
- Be aware that it is easy to reward the children who are most confident and skilled at mime, to the exclusion of others.
- Encourage discussion about the work, perhaps observing six to ten children working at the same time.

VARIATIONS OR DEVELOPMENTS:
If children find it difficult to mirror mimed actions, begin with mirroring abstract movements such as moving arms, legs, hands, nodding heads and so on. Other mimed sequences could include shaving, or putting on make-up; pulling faces in a larger mirror; trying on new clothes in a larger mirror; preparing for a party in a full-length mirror. Try the exercise in threes, with two people representing the mirror.

HALL OF MIRRORS

LEARNING OUTCOMES OR BENEFITS:
- Personal and social development: whole-group focus and concentration.
- Physical development: develops controlled, purposeful movement.
- Creative skills: requires instant imaginative responses.

WHERE?
School hall.

WHAT DO YOU NEED?
No specific equipment needed.

PROCESS:
1. Separate the class into two groups.
2. Ask one group to stand in a line, shoulder to shoulder.
3. Advise this group that they are to represent a fairground 'hall of mirrors'.
4. Inform the other group that they are to walk along the line, slowly looking into each mirror.
5. Tell the hall of mirrors that they must create distorted and grotesque mirror images of the 'visitors' who look into their mirrors.
6. Advise the mirrors that these images can be as realistic or grotesque as they wish.
7. Inform the visitors that they must move slowly enough along the line for each of them to be 'registered' by each mirror they look into.
8. Once the visitors have all walked along the line of mirrors, swap the two groups over and repeat the process, with mirrors now becoming visitors.

TEACHER GUIDANCE:
- This exercise causes great hilarity, but you should make clear that its aim is to explore physical representations and interpretations.
- Please ensure that this exercise is not used by the children as an opportunity to ridicule anyone because of their size or shape.
- Try to ensure that the distortions, while grotesque, are also fair.

Scholastic
DRAMA
Workshop

WHAT'S IN THE BAG?

LEARNING OUTCOMES OR BENEFITS:
- Creative skills: places an emphasis on using imaginative skills.
- Subject knowledge and understanding: (drama) develops basic performance skills; consolidates mime skills.
- Communication skills: develops vocabulary and descriptive language.
- Personal and social development: encourages a patient response; builds observation skills.

WHERE?
Classroom, circle area or school hall.

WHAT DO YOU NEED?
No specific equipment needed.

PROCESS:
1. Ask the children to sit in a circle.
2. Inform them that they must 'make believe' that they have all been given an imaginary bag.
3. Tell them that each of their imaginary bags contain something, and that only they know what that is.
4. Inform the children that they should let the rest of the class know what is in their imaginary bag by opening it and miming what is inside.
5. Advise the rest of the children that they must then try to guess what each imaginary bag contains.
6. Ask one child to begin the exercise by opening their bag and miming to the rest of the class what is inside it.
7. Ask the rest of the children to guess what the mystery object is from the mime performed.
8. Repeat the process of opening bags, miming and guessing either by choosing the children to perform their mime, or by asking for volunteers.

TEACHER GUIDANCE:
- Try to respond positively to each contribution.
- Be aware that this exercise can produce 'star performers', which can affect the confidence of others.

VARIATIONS OR DEVELOPMENTS:
When the children become more confident, ask them to take turns around the circle. Ask the children who are watching to comment on the mimes performed and reflect on how easy it was to recognize what was being produced from the bag.

Using the same process, explore the contents of an imaginary box and extend the mime skills by asking the children to unwrap the box first.

32

MAGIC MICROPHONE

LEARNING OUTCOMES OR BENEFITS:

- Communication skills: enables children to speak in more formal contexts; develops listening skills.
- Creative skills: encourages use of imaginative thoughts.
- Subject knowledge and understanding: (drama) provides initial experience of role-playing.

WHERE?

Classroom, circle area or school hall.

WHAT DO YOU NEED?

A suitable object to use as a 'magic microphone'.

PROCESS:

1. Sit with the children in a circle.
2. Show them the object you have chosen for your magic microphone.
3. Ask the children to imagine that the object is a magic microphone which they will all have the opportunity of speaking into.
4. Ensure that they all understand what a microphone is and what it does.
5. Tell the children that you will pass the magic microphone around the circle and that you want them to speak into it as if it were a real microphone.
6. Inform the children that they can each speak one sentence into the magic microphone, either making an announcement, introducing another child, making a statement about themselves or saying anything they wish.
7. Advise the children that if they cannot think of anything to say, they can miss their turn and hand the microphone on to their neighbour by simply saying 'pass'.
8. Hand the object to a child sitting next to you and allow it to travel around the circle.

TEACHER GUIDANCE:

- Take this exercise slowly. Many children will be nervous or concerned about 'getting it wrong' initially.
- Ensure that all contributions are praised and that no child feels a sense of failure for 'passing'.
- To help the children understand what is required of them, you could start the exercise by saying the first line into the microphone yourself.
- Choose your object carefully. A long ruler, comb or pencil works well as a magic microphone.

VARIATIONS OR DEVELOPMENTS:

Specify the sentences to be spoken by the children, for example introducing circus acts, introducing their friends, announcing the arrival of trains and so on.

Scholastic
DRAMA
Workshop

33

THE SENIOR CITIZEN

LEARNING OUTCOMES OR BENEFITS:

• Personal and social development: explores solving practical problems and dilemmas; prompts consideration of social responsibility; creates a whole-group focus.

• Communication skills: encourages children to classify and ask questions in a sensitive way.

• Subject knowledge and understanding: (drama) provides experience in responding to role as well as initial experience of hot-seating.

WHERE?

Classroom, circle area or school hall.

WHAT DO YOU NEED?

An item of costume or prop for your character (optional).

PROCESS:

1. Ask the children to sit in a circle or in their classroom places.
2. Now go 'into role' as an elderly person who cannot get out to the shops.
3. Introduce yourself to the children, giving your name and age, and explain that you have a problem which you'd like them to help you with.
4. In role, explain your difficulty in not being able to leave your house. Ask the children for their advice.
5. Encourage the children to ask any questions, and be prepared to respond to all of them!
6. Continue with the exercise until you feel a solution has been achieved and the children seem happy with the outcome.
7. Still in role, thank the children for their help and advice.
8. Come out of role and make sure that the children are aware that the exercise has ended.
9. Make a list of the children's ideas for future reference or following composition work.

TEACHER GUIDANCE:

• Plan and prepare your role carefully, thinking about any questions you may be asked and preparing the answers.

• Ensure that you emphasize that the purpose of the drama is to see if the children can help an elderly person.

• Avoid an acting sequence which portrays a comic, doddery old man or woman.

• You may use a shawl, walking stick or other effect to symbolize when you are in role, although these are not a necessity.

34

THE PARENT

LEARNING OUTCOMES OR BENEFITS:

- Personal and social development: helps children to reflect on their own family context; encourages children to give meaningful advice; enables children to share personal experiences.
- Subject knowledge and understanding: (drama) provides experience in responding to role and initial experience of role reversal – exploring a different perspective to a familiar problem – and hot-seating.
- Communication skills: encourages children to classify and ask pertinent questions.

WHERE?

Classroom, circle area or school hall.

WHAT DO YOU NEED?

Items of children's clothing as props.

PROCESS:

1. Ask the children to sit in a circle or in their classroom places.
2. Now go 'into role' as a parent who has two children, aged six and seven years, who will not tidy their bedrooms.
3. Introduce yourself to the children, giving your name and the names and ages of your children.
4. Use the items of clothing as props to explain and illustrate your problem to the children.
5. In role, tell the children of the attempts you have made to encourage your children to tidy their rooms.
6. Ask the children for their advice on what you can do to resolve your problem.
7. Encourage the children to ask any questions, and be prepared to respond to all of them!
8. Continue with the exercise until you feel a solution has been achieved and the children seem happy with the outcome.
9. Still in role, thank the children for their help and advice.
10. Come out of role and make sure that the children are aware that the exercise has ended.
11. Make a list of the children's suggestions and use this for future reference, or for composition work.

TEACHER GUIDANCE:

- Plan and prepare your role carefully, anticipating any questions you may be asked and preparing the answers.
- Ensure that you emphasize that the purpose of the drama is to explore a familiar problem from another perspective and to resolve the problem.
- Avoid using names for your 'children' which are familiar to the children in your class.
- You may use the items of clothing to indicate when you are 'in role', although this is not a necessity.

Scholastic
DRAMA
Workshop

Scholastic WORKSHOP

Chapter Five

THE MAGIC DOOR

INTRODUCTION

Project description

This is a short project which is based around the concept of imaginary or magic doors, and where they might lead to. The project develops progressively from children approaching different types of doors, to the more specific context of what might lay beyond the pictured 'magic door'.

Why this project?

This project is ideal as an introduction to basic drama methods and to encourage children to respond creatively. It develops their imagination and enables the children to experience the inventive process of drama in a non-threatening and enjoyable manner.

Length of project

Each activity session in this project, including the introductory session, is designed to be completed within 45 to 60 minutes. There are a total of four sessions, resulting in the complete project lasting approximately four hours. This could be completed over the period of half a term, or during one intensive week.

Project organization

The project is organized into five different sections:

- introductory session – establishes the subject context

- activity session 1 – 'Different doors'
- activity session 2 – 'Through the door'
- activity session 3 – 'The magic door'
- photocopiable resource.

Learning aims

- Subject knowledge and understanding: (drama) explores non-verbal communication.
- Creative development: encourages imaginative responses.
- Personal and social development: builds confidence and stimulates a whole-group approach.

Drama strategies

Much of the work centres upon a whole-group approach, using such methods as mime, creating sound effects and basic role-play. From this, more individual participation emerges through the use of small-group freezes and improvisation. Many of the drama conventions are utilized in their most basic form and enable the children to develop their skills and understanding at a gentle pace.

Resources needed

Very few resources are required for this project. These are: school hall, photocopiable page 82.

What the children do

Children mostly respond as themselves within an imaginary and creative context, learning gradually to role-play with increasing confidence. They will be expected to devise

Scholastic
DRAMA
Workshop

much of the drama work by responding to questions and guidance from the teacher and will learn to apply their responses to the dramatic context.

What the teacher does

The teacher will act as a guide and facilitate the development of the creative process, encouraging the increased individual participation of the children. The teacher is working out of role for much of the project, with a possible opportunity for being 'hot-seated' as a character in activity session 3. During this session the teacher will decide the direction and context of the drama, responding to suggestions from the children and will encourage development of the story. The most important aspect of the teacher's work during this project is to lead discussions, facilitating the development of the drama context and encouraging the children to feel a sense of ownership about the process.

Assessment

Follow-on exercises contained within this project should assist in the assessment of knowledge and skills gained. Use the assessment section of this book for recording achievements (see pages 13–20). Link assessment to the *Desirable Outcomes for Children's Learning* or KS1 level indicators.

INTRODUCTORY SESSION

Resources needed

School hall.

What to do

Sit with the children in a circle. Explain that you are going to work together as a whole group to create different sound effects. Tell the children that you will give them the title of the noise that you want them to create and that they should then respond by making that noise. Work through the following list:
- an aeroplane flying
- a cat meowing
- someone drinking a mug of soup
- a train pulling out of a station
- a baby crying
- a door creaking slowly open
- a door slamming shut.

Praise each effort and repeat any sound effects which you feel could be improved.

Now ask the children: *What other sound effects could we do about doors?* Possible suggestions could be:
- someone knocking on a door
- someone turning a key in a lock
- someone ringing a doorbell
- someone rattling a door handle
- a door creaking slowly open (again)
- a door being closed gently
- a door slamming shut (again).

Encourage the children to try making these sound effects in a variety of ways, not just with their voices but using other parts of their bodies or their surroundings. Praise all efforts.

Tell the children that you are now going to ask some of them to mime being a door which others can open and walk through. Inform the children that others in the class will provide the sound effects of the door being opened and closed and the remainder will actually walk through the door.

Nominate four or five children to create your door with their bodies and stand them in a space in the hall. 'Sculpt' them into position, until you have a door frame and a recognizable door which can be opened and closed and which moves in unison. Choose eight or ten other children to sit in a space at the side and ask them to provide the accompanying sound effects for the door being opened and, finally, closed. Line the remaining children up and tell them that they will be walking through the door.

Advise those children creating the accompanying sound effects to watch the movements carefully and respond in sound to the door being opened and closed. Ensure that everyone is ready to start and that all are clear about what is expected of them, then ask the first child in the line to slowly open the door and walk through, followed by the rest of the line until the final child slowly closes the door behind him or her.

Repeat the process two or three times, refining the movements and sounds, adding sounds – such as knocking on the door – and swapping children around so that as many as possible experience the different aspects of the process.

Thank the children for their efforts and advise them that you will be continuing with this theme during the next session – this will provide reassurance for those children who feel that they didn't play a major role during this session.

1

DIFFERENT DOORS

OBJECTIVES

Introduces the children to basic mime and expressive movement methods within the project context.

RESOURCES:

School hall.

GROUP SIZE:

Individual participation within whole-group context.

STAGE 1:

Sit with the children in a circle and initiate a recap discussion on the activities they experienced in the introductory session. Inform them: *Today you are going to imagine lots of different types of doors and I am going to ask you to open them in different ways.*

Tell the children to stand in a space in the hall and say to them: *Imagine that there is a door in front of you.* Ask them to look carefully at their door and to decide exactly what it looks like: its size, what it is made of, where the handle is, whether it has a doorbell or a knocker, where the lock is, whether it has a letterbox, what colour it is, and so on. Allow plenty of time for the children to respond to these different criteria, introducing them one at a time and pausing to enable the children to create their door in their imagination.

Once you feel that the children can all 'see' their door, say: *Your door is locked. I want you to find the door key in your pocket, unlock your door, open it and step through it. All right? Off you go.* Watch this mime sequence until all of the children have completed it and then ask them to reverse the process – stepping out of the door, closing it and locking it behind them. Praise all efforts.

You could ask some of the more confident and able children to show their sequence to the rest of the group.

Now tell the children: *In front of you is a strange door that you haven't seen before. You want to go through it but the door seems to be locked. Try to open your door by pushing it or pulling on the handle.*

Allow this mime process to continue for a few moments and then say: *Look around to see if you can find a key to open this door.* Again, pause while this mime takes place, and then add: *Try one more time to open the strange door by using the handle. It still won't open. Now stand back and look at your door to see if there is a doorbell you could ring or a knocker you could use. If there is, ring the bell or use the door knocker.* Allow time for the children to complete their final mime. Praise all efforts.

STAGE 2:

Now tell the children: *This time I want you to imagine different types of doors and to open and go through each of them.* Ask the children to mime 'seeing', opening and/or going through different doors from a selection of your choice.

Scholastic
DRAMA
Workshop

These could include:
- a tatty old door that's falling apart
- a door with the handle very high up on it
- a door with the handle very low down
- a revolving door
- a heavy metal door
- a very small door
- a very narrow door.

Allow time for each mime and increase the time allowed as the children become more proficient at the process and more confident about the concept of miming. Praise all efforts and thank the children for their contributions. After you have worked through all of your own ideas, ask the children for suggestions of other door shapes to try.

You could ask some of the more confident and able children to show their mimes to the rest of the group.

Once the children have completed all of the mimes suggested, ask them to sit in a circle with you again, and initiate a discussion on the effectiveness of mimes by asking questions such as: *How could we tell that someone was walking through a tatty old door? How did you show that the door was very narrow? What's the difference between a revolving door and another type of door? How can we show that by just using our bodies? What do we have to do with our bodies and faces to show other people that the door is a heavy one?*

You should aim to reach the conclusion that ideas can be expressed clearly without having to use any sort of verbal communication. Thank the children for their contributions and ask them to stand in a space in the hall again.

STAGE 3:
Tell the children: *Now I would like you to show me how you feel about going through doors which lead to different places.* Ask the children to mime opening and going through doors which lead to specific areas. Some examples could be:
- the door into school
- the door into the dentist's
- the door into a sweet shop
- the door into your house
- the door into the toy shop
- the door into the doctor's.

Place the emphasis on the children showing how they feel in their facial expressions and body language when going through each different door. Again some children could be asked to demonstrate their mimes to the rest of the group.

Add any ideas of your own, or ask for additional suggestions from the children. Encourage the children to think carefully about their mimes by praising particularly good efforts. Once each mime has been completed, thank the children for their work and ask them to sit in a circle with you again.

Conclude with a final discussion about the techniques the children used to express how they felt about going through each particular door, by using questions such as: *What did you do with your faces to show when you were happy about where you were going? How did you show with your bodies that you were unhappy about going through the door?*

Thank the children for their contributions, inform them that you will continue with this theme during the next session and ensure that they understand that this session has now ended.

FOLLOW-UP ACTIVITIES:

Ask the children to:

- draw a picture of their original imaginary door, paying great attention to detail
- draw a picture of themselves going through one of the doors in stage 3, showing their feelings clearly
- write a descriptive piece about their imaginary door.

2
THROUGH THE DOOR

OBJECTIVES:

Consolidates expressive movement skills and encourages creative responses.

RESOURCES:

School hall.

GROUP SIZE:

Whole group and individual work.

STAGE 1:

Sit with the children in a circle and lead a brief recap discussion about the activities they experienced in the previous session and the skills and knowledge they gained. Inform the children: *Today I am going to ask you to imagine that you can see different things when you open your doors and I want you to show me how you feel about what you find when you open your doors.*

Ask the children to find a space in the hall and to stand in it. Tell them: *Imagine that you have a door in front of you.* Advise the children that you will ask them to open their imaginary doors and will tell them what they find when they are opened. Ask them to react to what is behind their doors, using their faces, bodies and voices. Choose various options for this exercise. These could include:

- seeing a beautiful garden
- seeing a large fire-breathing dragon
- seeing a huge bowl of ice-cream
- seeing a big spider
- seeing all your family and friends waiting for you
- seeing a long, dark, spooky tunnel.

The group should react all at the same time to each idea which you give. Allow a pause after each reaction to enable the children to complete their responses fully and to close the door again. Praise their efforts, particularly any children who are reacting effectively.

Once all of the ideas have been exhausted, thank the children for their efforts and ask them to sit in a group at one side of the hall.

Scholastic
DRAMA
Workshop

STAGE 2:

Tell the children that now you are going to ask for volunteers to stand in front of the group, open their imaginary door and react to something they see behind it, and that the rest of you are going to try to guess what that person has seen.

Either nominate a child or choose a volunteer to stand in front of the others. Advise this child to think of what could be behind their imaginary door but to keep it to themselves for now. Allow a brief pause while the volunteer thinks of what lies behind their door. Then say: *Are you ready? Have you thought of what is behind your door when you open it? Can you show everyone else what it is by the way you behave when you open your door? Good. Now open your door.*

These individual mimes will often be very quick and you may have to ask children to repeat them. They will also often be difficult to guess, or the individuals concerned may simply latch on to an answer without it necessarily being the correct one! All of these issues are really quite irrelevant; the main idea is that children gain confidence in working in front of others and that they learn through observing as an audience.

Repeat this mime and guessing process with as many children in the group as possible and thank each volunteer for their contribution. Continue until no more children want to volunteer.

STAGE 3:

Sit in front of the children and tell them: *Now I want you to imagine that in this space in this hall is a magic door and whoever steps through it can become something or someone else. Look, I'll show you.* Stand in the centre of the room, facing the children. Open your imaginary door and step through it, saying as you do so: *I step through the door and I become...* (Insert whatever you like here, for example a famous film star... an angry giant... a beautiful butterfly.) Ensure that you illustrate your new persona with facial expressions and actions, too!

Invite each child in turn to stand in front of the group and to step through the imaginary door and 'become' something or someone else. Allow a pause to enable the 'audience' to acknowledge each contribution. Praise all efforts and thank each child after their 'performance'.

You must insist on silence and the full attention of the audience for each child's contribution. Some children will be reluctant to take part, but a little gentle encouragement and a suggestion of what they could become will usually overcome this. Some children may want to go twice – if you have the time then positively encourage this enthusiasm!

Once each child has stepped through the 'magic' door, gather all of the children together in a circle again and conclude with a final discussion, placing the emphasis on the 'magic' aspect of the door and how wonderful its special powers are. Thank the children for their efforts, inform them that this theme of magic doors will be continued in the next session and ensure that they understand that this session has now ended.

FOLLOW-UP ACTIVITIES:

Ask the children to:
- draw two pictures – before and after they stepped through the magic door
- write an account of the session
- draw a picture of the magic door.

THE MAGIC DOOR

OBJECTIVES:
Further develops imaginative responses through the creation of the drama and consolidates skills.

RESOURCES:
School hall, photocopiable page 82.

GROUP SIZE:
Whole group, small group and individual work.

STAGE 1:
Sit in a circle with the children. Initiate a brief recap discussion about the activities from the previous session, in particular highlighting the concept of the magic door. Show the children the door picture (photocopiable page 82) and ask them questions such as: *Where does this door lead to? Is it a magic door? Do the two parts of the door lock? Is the door locked now, and if so, why? Who owns the keys and where are they? What is behind the door? What would happen to you if you went through the door? Would you like to go through the door? Who would you meet if you went through the door? What would you see if you went through the door?*

Use the discussion to create a definite image of the magic door (if it is magic): how it can be opened, where it leads to, what could be behind it and what would happen if you stepped through it. Decide as a group on one idea which tells the complete story of the door in the picture. Once this has been achieved, tell the children: *I want you to imagine that this door is in this room and I will ask you to tell our story of people seeing the door, opening it and going through it.*

This is where your role as director of the drama is paramount. You have created the story in negotiation with the children and now have to ensure that every piece of action which follows expresses that story as it has been agreed.

Ask the children to form small groups of four or five and instruct them to find a space in the hall to work in. Inform them that each group will tell the story of the door from the picture, as it has been agreed. Advise each group that they must imagine that they each have the door in their own particular space.

Tell the children that the first thing they must do is decide where their door is, to mime finding the door, trying to open it, looking for and finding the key and, finally, choosing one of the group to actually unlock the door.

Tell them that as soon as every group has unlocked their door, you will instruct the whole group to 'freeze' and that will be the signal for everyone to be completely still and silent. Allow the children a few moments to absorb this information and to discuss and negotiate roles among themselves.

Ensure that everyone is clear about what is expected of them and then say: *Is everyone ready? All right, off you go.* Watch carefully for every group to complete its mime and, once this has been achieved, give the 'Freeze' command. Praise their efforts.

Scholastic
DRAMA
Workshop

STAGE 2:

Advise the children that now you want them to think about how they would all feel before they opened the door. Instruct them to create a short improvisation based upon the discussion the group might have about opening the door and its potential consequences. Allow a short while for planning and preparation and move around the room, monitoring progress. When you feel that all of the children understand what is expected of them, ask them to begin with their improvisations. Allow these to continue until you can see that each group has reached a point where the only next move is to actually go through the door, and then give the 'Freeze' command again.

At this point say: *You are all ready to step through the door. What I would like you to do is to open your door very slowly, step through it and then quickly freeze in positions which show how you feel about what you find.* When you feel that all of the children understand what is expected of them, say: *Are you all ready to step through your doors? All right, step through them.* Praise their efforts.

At this stage, children should be expressing their ideas and reactions very well. You should now allow each group to show the rest of the class their ideas, and use positive language to encourage each effort.

STAGE 3:

Inform the children that as the last person stepped through the door, it suddenly slammed shut behind them and locked itself! Tell them that you want them to act out what they all did and said when that happened.

This final stage will depend on what has been decided lies beyond the door: if it's something pleasant, the children will quite happily remain locked in, if not, they will have to react in a completely different manner, possibly trying to escape or protect one another. Again, lead the drama in the right direction.

Allow each group a few moments to discuss and prepare their role-playing, moving around the room to clarify that each child understands what they have to do, and then ensure that all the children are in their 'frozen' positions just inside the door, and repeat the line again: *As the last person stepped through the door, it suddenly slammed shut behind them and locked itself!* Allow the improvisations to continue for a few moments to enable each child to participate fully. Give the 'Freeze' command again to stop the action and then ask each group to show its improvisation to the rest. Praise all efforts.

Ask the children to sit in a circle again and lead a final discussion which should conclude the story, asking the children to decide 'What happened next?' Acknowledge all responses, but make no final choice with regards to the outcome of the story. Thank the children for their efforts and ensure that they understand that the session, and the project, is now ended.

FOLLOW-UP ACTIVITIES:

Ask the children to:
• write the ending of the story
• tell, in pictures, their story of the magic door
• draw a picture of what was behind their door.

As a class:
• Read an extract from *Alice's Adventures in Wonderland*, the section where Alice tries to get through the door, and use it as a basis for another 'What happened next?' story.

THE MAGIC DOOR

Scholastic
DRAMA
Workshop

Scholastic
WORKSHOP

Chapter Six

THE PRINCESS WHO WOULDN'T SMILE

INTRODUCTION

Project description

This project is based on the poem 'The Princess Who Wouldn't Smile' by Clive Riche. It explores the poem in depth, while also providing opportunities for linked drama and creative work. It is a good example of how a stimulus can be used as a basis for drama work, and it provides a basic introduction to text-based performance.

Why this project?

This project enables the children to understand the concept of creating images from words and facilitates the opportunity for creative development around a central theme. It is a simple, non-threatening introduction to both analytical and performance skills and allows the children to experience a variety of drama methods.

Length of project

Each activity session in this project, including the introductory session, is designed to be completed within 45 to 60 minutes. There are six sessions, so the project lasts approximately six hours. It could be completed, with associated follow-on work, either over the period of a whole term or during one intensive week.

Project organization

The project is organized into the following sections:

- introductory session – establishes the subject context
- activity session 1 – 'Exploring verses 1 and 2'
- activity session 2 – 'Exploring verses 3 and 4'
- activity session 3 – 'Exploring verses 5, 6 and 7'
- activity session 4 – 'Exploring verses 8, 9 and 10'
- activity session 5 – 'The complete poem' (performing the whole poem)
- photocopiable resources.

Learning aims

- Subject knowledge and understanding: (English) in-depth exploration of text; a basic approach to character analysis; (drama) introduces a variety of drama methods; develops performance skills.
- Personal and social development: develops listening skills; builds cognitive and analytical abilities; encourages appropriate creative responses.

Drama strategies

In the initial stages the drama centres around a whole-group approach through such methods as role-on-the-wall, group discussion, movement and mime. Individual participation is gradually increased and the middle sessions centre around small-group work through freezes and role-play in a performance context. The teacher is hot-seated in role as the princess in activity session 3, but remains out of role for all other sessions during the project.

Resources needed

Access to school hall or similar large space; a large sheet of paper (lining wallpaper cut to a five-foot length and flattened out); chairs; large display board; photocopiable pages 101–106, writing and drawing materials.

What the children do

Children respond as themselves during discussions and text analysis and should be encouraged to develop their memory skills through recall of specific aspects of the poem. They then participate in role as each verse is brought to life, culminating in a complete performance of the poem in the final session. Children work together to move the drama forward by devising and illustrating creative responses to requests and questions from the teacher.

What the teacher does

The teacher must prepare thoroughly by reading and knowing the poem and seeing its potential for both character analysis and performance. He or she then directs the drama work, guiding the children as they explore each section of the poem. Children should be allowed the opportunity to both ask and respond to questions about the poem and its contents, enabling them to feel a stronger sense of ownership about their work. The teacher responds in role during hot-seating in activity session 3.

Assessment

Text appreciation is assessed through exercises completed both during and after the drama. Assessment of children's understanding of the poem content is ongoing and should be

Scholastic **DRAMA** Workshop

revealed during the activity sessions. The assessment section of this book should be used for recording achievements (see pages 13–20). Link assessment to the *Desirable Outcomes for Children's Learning* or KS1 level indicators.

INTRODUCTORY SESSION

Resources needed

Photocopiable pages 101–105; large sheet of paper; paper for drawing; writing and drawing materials.

What to do

Ask the children to sit in their classroom places or in the quiet corner. Distribute copies of the poem (photocopiable pages 101–105) and read it to them while they follow the text.

Initiate a discussion about the poem, asking the children to consider and respond to such questions as: *Why doesn't the princess smile? How do her parents try to help her? How would you try to make her smile? What do you think would make her smile? What story does the poem tell us? Where does the story happen? When does it happen? How do the different people try to make the princess smile? Why don't they work? Who is successful, and why?*

Prepare and ask additional questions which will aid basic understanding of the story, for example asking what the town crier might have said, what the poster about the contest would have said.

Check the children's level of comprehension by asking them to define or explain certain words if they can, considering them in the context of the poem, for example 'nigh' (verse 1); 'rehearsed' (verse 4); 'renowned' (verse 4); 'mirth' (verse 5); 'allotted' (verse 6); 'suitors' (verse 7); 'drained' (verse 7). Then give the correct definition of each word yourself.

The aim is to discuss the poem content as much as possible and to provide a strong base for later exploration. Children will begin to place the poem in a subjective context, and may relate the content to personal feelings and experiences by telling their own stories – this should be encouraged.

Once the discussion is completed, take the large sheet of paper and a marker pen. Choose a small child and ask him or her to lie down on the sheet of paper with arms at the side and feet together. It is probably advisable to choose a girl, as boys may feel embarrassed about being a princess! Draw around the outline, being as careful as possible to create a recognizable 'human' shape and taking care not to touch any clothing with the marker pen! The aim is to have a body outline to use for a 'role-on-the-wall' activity. Children will find this process hysterically funny and may direct their laughter at the child you have chosen to draw around. Make sure the volunteer does not feel humiliated by praising stillness and stressing the importance of participation.

Once you have drawn your outline, thank the volunteer and tell the children: *This shape is the princess in the poem. Can we think of some ideas, thoughts, facts and feelings about the princess to write in the shape?* Explain that on the inside of the princess outline, you will write words that show how the princess feels and behaves. (Possible examples are 'sad', 'solemn', 'won't smile'.) In the space around the outside of the princess shape, you will write words which give facts about her and say what makes her feel and behave the way she does. (Possible examples are 'pale-skinned', 'slender hands', 'talented', 'beautiful', 'graceful', '22 years old', 'her sadness makes her parents unhappy', 'her father wants her to marry'.) It doesn't matter too much if words end up in the 'wrong' place – the aim is to discuss the character in detail.

Take your time to complete this 'role-on-the-wall', allowing as many children as possible to contribute. Put every contribution on the paper, whether you feel it is relevant or not. When you feel that all possible responses have been exhausted, or that the children are becoming restless, stop the activity and thank them for their excellent ideas.

Label the outline of the princess, then secure it on the display board – if there is enough space on the wall, place it in a vertical position, if not, then lying it down on a flat surface will suffice.

Thank the children for their work and advise them that the session is now at an end but that you will be continuing with the story of the princess who would not smile during the next session.

1

EXPLORING VERSES 1 AND 2

OBJECTIVES:
To begin exploring the narrative of the poem in depth.

RESOURCES:
School hall; photocopiable pages 101–105; paper; drawing materials.

GROUP SIZE:
Whole group, small groups, pairs and individual work.

STAGE 1:
Sit with the children in a circle and say: *Now we're going to read just the first two verses of 'The Princess Who Would Not Smile', which we read last time.* Distribute copies of the poem (photocopiable pages 101–105) and read the two verses while the children follow. Then ask: *Can we decide on three important things that happen in these verses?*

Lead the discussion so that the following three images emerge as the important ones:

1 what the princess does – she dances, sings, plays the spoons, whistles

2 what the nursemaid did to upset the king when the princess was small – she said that the princess was ugly

3 what the king did as a result – banishing all mirrors from the palace.

Tell the children that you want them to create 'frozen' pictures of these three images from the poem.

Start with image 1. Divide half the class into pairs, one in each pair to play the king, the other to play the princess. Designate a specific area in the hall for the freeze to be created in. Instruct the children playing the princess to 'freeze' in one of her activities. The other child in each pair should create a freeze that shows the king's reaction. 'Sculpt' the children until they are all in relevant positions and then count down from three and give the 'Freeze' command. Hold the freeze for a few seconds, then thank the children and instruct them to relax.

Ask the other half of the class to make (constructive) comments about the freezes.

Scholastic
DRAMA
Workshop

Then using the half of the class who have been watching and making comments, repeat the procedure to create freezes of image 2. This time one child in each pair should be the nursemaid who comments on the royal baby, perhaps bending over the princess lying in a crib or cradle, or holding the child in her arms.

For image 3, all the children should work individually to create a freeze of the king 'in a fury', issuing his command.

Make sure you count down from three each time and give the 'Freeze' command clearly, praising stillness and thanking the children afterwards as you tell them to relax.

STAGE 2:

Now ask the children to find a partner and a space to work in. If you have an odd number of children in your group, make one of the pairs a 'three'. Tell them that you want them to imagine that they are courtiers talking to each other about the princess: what might they say about her?

Allow a few seconds for the children to understand what is expected of them and to prepare their ideas, and then say: 'All right, courtiers, off you go.' While the conversations are taking place, walk around the room, listening and giving positive encouragement. Let the conversations continue for about 2 or 3 minutes and then praise the children for their efforts and ask them to find a space to work in alone.

Next, say to the children: *Now I want you to imagine that you are the princess who wouldn't smile. You need to mime (that means silently!) what she does: she dances, sings, plays the spoons and whistles tunes. But remember – she does all these very solemnly; she doesn't seem to be enjoying herself!* Ensure that all the children understand what is expected of them and then ask them to continue with their mimes.

You can focus their actions by providing a commentary, saying: *Here is the princess in her lovely palace, so talented and beautiful. She enjoys dancing… singing… playing the spoons… whistling… I wonder why she looks so sad.* Encourage the children to match their mimes to your words. Praise all efforts and then ask the children to sit with you in a circle again.

STAGE 3:

Say to the children: *Now we are going to make the freezes again from the beginning. This time we're going to bring the pictures to life with silent movements (mime) while I read the verses.*

Choose children, as before, to represent the princess and the king and ask them to position themselves in 'frozen' image 1. Ask them to hold the freeze as you start reading the verse and then to use mime to bring it to life when they hear the line 'She danced, she sang, she played…'

Choose children to be the nursemaid and the baby for image 2 and ask them to begin their actions when they hear 'when these words did flow…'

Finally, for image 3, all the children should start being the king when they hear 'To protect his daughter…'

Ensure that the children are aware that their actions should be silent and understand what is expected of them. Allow a brief period before starting to discuss how their mimes could be performed effectively. Then work through each verse, nominating different children each time to start with a freeze of their image, to bring their image to life with mime at the appropriate point in the text, and to do this while listening carefully to your accompanying narration of each verse.

Encourage those children not performing to be the audience and to observe the others quietly.

Once you have 'frozen', brought to life and read each of the two verses, thank and praise the children for their efforts and inform them that the session is now ended, but that you will be continuing with the story of the princess who would not smile during the next session.

FOLLOW-UP ACTIVITIES:
Ask the children to:
• draw each of the 'frozen' images they created
• write captions for their drawings of the 'frozen' images.

EXPLORING VERSES 3 AND 4

OBJECTIVES:
To develop mime and movement skills and create physical representations of the verses.

RESOURCES:
School hall; photocopiable pages 101–105; paper; writing and drawing materials.

GROUP SIZE:
Whole group, pairs, small groups and individual work.

STAGE 1:
Ask the children to sit in a circle, and distribute copies of the poem (photocopiable pages 101–105). Tell the children that today they are going to concentrate on verses 3 and 4 of 'The Princess Who Wouldn't Smile'. Read through verses 3 and 4 while the children follow.

Initiate a brief discussion about the events of the verses and ask: *What three important things happen in these verses?*
Lead the children towards identifying the following three events:
1 The king asks, 'What can we do?' And the princess thinks of her answer.
2 The town crier announces the smiling contest.
3 The young men practise their tricks to make the princess smile.

Tell the children that, as with the verses explored in the previous session, they are

Scholastic
DRAMA
Workshop

going to create freezes of the images.

Ask the children to find a partner and a space to work in. Tell them to create a freeze to show the king and the princess in image 1. Ensure that they all understand what is expected of them and then give a countdown from three followed by the command to 'freeze'.

Now ask all the children individually to create a freeze which represents image 2, giving the same countdown and 'Freeze' command.

Repeat the process with image 3. Remind them of the different tricks and ask each child to choose one to represent as a freeze. Ask the children to hold all freezes for a brief moment and then praise all efforts and allow them to relax.

STAGE 2:

Tell the children: *Now we'll begin to bring the verses to life with movement. Think of some movements to mime the king and the princess, the town crier and the young men.* Ensure that they understand that mime is movement without sound.

You can focus their actions by providing a commentary, saying: *The king sighs, 'What can we do? The princess thinks hard, the town crier announces the contest and young men practise their tricks to make the princess smile.* Encourage the children to match their actions to your words. Take it slowly and ensure all are participating.

Praise all efforts and then, when this mime process has been completed, ask the children to form groups of four to six people and to find a space to work in. Tell them that now you want them to think about the chorus – 'the verse that is repeated several times'. Remind them of the words and ask them to come up with actions to match, for example beseeching with hands together for the phrase 'Oh dearest princess', smiling on the word 'smile' and looking solemn on 'sad'.

Then ask: *Can you think of some sounds to go with your movements?* Allow time for the groups to plan and prepare their movements, moving around the room to provide assistance wherever it is required. Then ask each group to show their movements in turn. Respond positively to each demonstration.

Tell the children that you will now read out the chorus and that you want them all to respond with their movements when they hear the words 'dearest', 'smile' and 'sad'. Ensure that everyone is clear about what is expected of them and then read through the chorus slowly once, allowing the children time to perform their movements. Praise their efforts. Ask the children to sit in a circle with you again.

STAGE 3:

Inform the children that, as before, you are now going to bring these two verses to life. Advise them that they will perform verses 2 and 3 and then go straight into their groups to perform the chorus. Ask the children to find a space to work in which is close to the other members of their group.

Instruct the children to listen very carefully as you read the poem and ask them to begin with their freeze of the king sighing deeply. Tell them that they are to then start miming all the actions representing the movements of the king, the princess and the town crier.

Advise the children that, as soon as they have completed their mimes of the town crier, they are to move into their groups to perform their movements for the chorus. Ensure that all of the children understand what is expected of them and then read through verse 3.

Take the reading as slowly as you can without it sounding ridiculous and, however well or badly this goes, make sure that you praise and thank the children for their efforts.

Inform the children that this session has now ended, but advise them that you will be exploring the story of the princess who would not smile again during the next session.

FOLLOW-UP ACTIVITIES:

Ask the children to:
- write speech bubbles for the princess, king and town crier from verse 3
- draw the town crier
- write some of the bad jokes for the princess
- draw some of the young men doing their tricks to make the princess smile
- draw each of the 'frozen' images they created (as in activity session 1)
- write a caption underneath their drawings of the 'frozen' images (as in activity session 1).

Scholastic
DRAMA
Workshop

EXPLORING VERSES 5, 6 AND 7

OBJECTIVES:
To consolidate movement skills and explore the poem in more depth.

RESOURCES:
School hall; photocopiable pages 101–105; chair; role-on-the-wall created in the introductory session (see page 85); paper, writing and drawing materials.

GROUP SIZE:
Whole group in pairs, small groups and individual work.

STAGE 1:
Sit with the children in a circle and hand out copies of the poem (photocopiable pages 101–105). Read through verses 5, 6 and 7 while the children follow. Tell them: *Now we are going to look closely at these verses. What three important things happen in this part?* Then direct a brief discussion about the contents of each of the verses and the images contained within them. Draw out the following three images:

1 the king and queen kneeling at prayer
2 suitors failing in the contest
3 the two ten-second attempts from Nincom and Poop.

Inform the children that, as with the verses explored in the previous session, they are going to create freezes of these images and then bring the verses to life. Ask the children to find a space to work in, in pairs, and tell each pair to create a freeze which represents image 1 of the king and queen praying for help. Ensure that they all understand what is expected of them and then give a countdown from three, followed by the command to 'Freeze'.

Now ask each pair to create a freeze which represents image 2. They should each choose one of the suitors in the contest – give the same countdown and 'Freeze!' command.

Finally, repeat the process with image 3, with one of the pair being Nincom and the other taking Poop's role. Ask the children to hold all of their freezes for a brief moment, and then praise all efforts and allow them to relax.

STAGE 2:
Inform the children that they are now going to bring the verses to life with movement. Ask them to mime the movements of the king and queen (remaining in their individual spaces), the suitors

at the contest and then Nincom and Poop. Ensure that they appreciate that mime is movement without sound.

You can focus their actions by providing a commentary, saying: *The king and queen pray for help. They only want their daughter to be happy. All the suitors try their very best to make the princess smile, with tricks and jokes, but – no smile. Finally, Nincom and Poop do their tricks… still no smile from the princess.* Encourage the children to match their actions to your words.

Praise all efforts and then, when the mime process has been completed, ask the children to form groups of four to six and to find a space to work in. Tell them that, as in the previous session, you want them to devise a movement to represent the chorus. Inform the children that sounds can also be incorporated to support their movements.

Allow a short period of time for the groups to plan and prepare their movements. This should be easier if they have completed earlier activity sessions. When you think they are ready, ask each of the groups to demonstrate the movement they have devised to the others. Respond in a positive manner to each demonstration.

Divide the class into three and give each group a 'chorus part', for example the first group should come up with a movement for the word 'dearest', the second group for the word 'smile' and the third group for the word 'sad'. Allow a few minutes for the groups to work on their movements.

Now say to the children: *I'm going to read out the chorus and when you hear me say the word for your chorus part, I want you to perform your movement.* Ensure that the children are clear about what is expected of them and then read through the chorus slowly, allowing the children the time to perform their movements. Praise their efforts and ask the children to sit in a circle with you again.

STAGE 3:

Tell the children that, as before, they are going to bring the verses to life. Explain that first they are going to perform the movements for verses 5, 6 and 7 individually and then form into their small groups to perform the movements for each chorus.

Ask the children to find a space to work in which is close to the other members of their group. Instruct them to listen very carefully as you read the verses and ask them to begin with their freeze of the king and queen at prayer. Inform them that they are to then start miming all the actions representing the movements when they hear you say, 'On the eve of

Scholastic
DRAMA
Workshop

the smiling contest day…'

Tell the children that, as soon as they have completed their mimes, they are to move into their small groups to perform the chorus. Ensure that they all understand what is expected of them, and then read through verses 5, 6 and 7.

Children should work through these procedures much more quickly now, having already experienced them in previous sessions. Try taking the reading a little faster to develop their listening skills and the speed of their responses. However well or badly this exercise goes, make sure that you praise the children for their efforts.

Once the three verses have been brought to life, ask the children to sit in a circle with you again. Bring down the 'role-on-the-wall' from the display and then sit on your 'hot-seating' chair in front of the children.

Inform them that they are to imagine that you are the princess and that they now have the opportunity to ask any questions they like to find out more information from you. Go into role, using your posture, facial expression and voice and saying: *I am the princess – what would you like to ask me?* Respond to all questions in role, answering as carefully, clearly and honestly as you can.

Children will be hesitant at first, but will soon be firing questions at you rapidly! Some less confident children may repeat questions already asked – this is their way of joining in without pressure – simply repeat the answer given previously! Make sure that you have prepared as much as possible in advance for any questions you might be asked, although most of your responses will have to be spontaneous. Don't be afraid to refuse to answer any questions, or to throw the answer back to the children by saying: *I don't know – what do you think?*

Continue the hot-seating process until you have built up a more comprehensive picture of the princess, and stop before the children get bored. Come out of role by standing up and changing the 'hot seating' chair for another one.

Now ask the children to look at the 'role-on-the-wall' completed at the beginning of the project. Say: *I think we have learned a lot more about the princess from your questions. Can we use our new knowledge to add or change anything on this?* (Indicate the role-on-the-wall.) Using a different coloured marker pen from the one you used originally, add words or phrases, or change them, on the role-on-the-wall, asking the children to offer suggestions. Once all ideas have been exhausted, thank the children for their contributions and praise their efforts. Finally, inform the children that this session has now ended, but advise them that you will continue with your exploration of the story of the princess who would not smile during the next session.

FOLLOW-UP ACTIVITIES:
Ask the children to:
• draw a picture of the princess
• write a description of the princess and to give her a name!
• draw a picture of each of their 'frozen' images (as in previous sessions)
• write a caption for each of their frozen image drawings (as in previous sessions).

4
EXPLORING VERSES 8, 9 AND 10

OBJECTIVES:
To consolidate movement and performance skills through exploration of verses 8, 9 and 10.

RESOURCES:
School hall; photocopiable pages 101–105; paper; writing materials.

GROUP SIZE:
Whole group, small groups and individual work.

STAGE 1:
Sit with the children in a circle and hand out copies of the poem (photocopiable pages 101–105). Read through verses 8, 9 and 10 while the children follow. Advise them that you will be exploring these final verses of the poem during the session, then initiate a brief discussion about the contents of each verse and the three important images contained within them:

1 'Firsten Last' announcing his intention to make the princess smile
2 the princess singing as Firsten steps into the ring with his mirror
3 the princess smiling hugely and in a prolonged manner!

Inform the children that, as previously, they are going to create freezes of these images and then bring the three verses to life. Ask the children to form small groups of six to ten and to find a space to work in. It would be advisable during this session to form the

groups yourself and to nominate children to play specific roles. Much of the time can be lost by children's lack of ability to negotiate parts fairly and some individual representation of the character of Firsten Last is central to the work during this session.

Instruct the groups to each create a freeze which represents the image of a group of courtiers looking on as the child representing Firsten Last freezes in the position of announcing his intention 'with his hand'. Ensure that all of the groups understand what is expected of them and allow a brief time for preparation and positioning before giving the countdown from three followed by the command to 'Freeze'.

Now ask the children to create a freeze which shows Firsten standing in the ring with his mirror while the princess sings her song. The remaining group should represent the courtiers, all holding their breath and looking on with great anticipation. Again, allow a short time for preparation before giving the same countdown and 'Freeze' command.

Finally, ask the children to find a space to work in alone and ask them to 'freeze' as image 3 – the princess reacting to Firsten's trick. Ask the children to hold all of their freezes for a brief moment, then praise all efforts and allow them to relax.

STAGE 2:

Inform the children that, as before, they are now going to bring each of the verses to life with mime. Ask them to form into their small groups again and find a space to work in. Instruct the children to perform a mime of Firsten's arrival at the contest. Ensure that the children appreciate that mime is movement without sound. Allow the mimes to continue for a few moments and then stop the action. At this stage, if you have sufficient time, you could ask each group to show their mime to the others, remembering to thank them and praise their efforts after each one.

Now ask the children to find a space in which to work individually and instruct them to perform a mime of Firsten stepping into the ring waving his mirror. Again, some individuals could be asked to show their mimes to the others. Praise all efforts.

Remind the children that the next verse to be brought to life is the chorus and ask them to recap how they have previously brought this to life. Ask them, in unison this time, to practise their movements to represent the chorus. Tell them they can use sounds to support their movements if they wish.

Allow a short period of time for the groups to plan and prepare their movements and, when you think they are ready, ask each of the groups to demonstrate the movements they have devised to the others. Respond positively to each demonstration.

Try not to insist that any of these movements are the same as those the children have devised in previous sessions. There should be no sense imposed of the 'right' way to do this and children should feel free to change or refine their previous creations, or to re-create them.

Advise the children to remember these movements because they will not perform them again until the end of the activity session. Ask the children to return to their original groups and to find a space to work in.

Tell them that they are now going to perform a mime of Firsten's trick. Again, instruct them that mimes should be performed without sound. Permit the groups a few moments for planning and preparation, ensure that all of the children understand what is expected of them and then ask them to begin their mimes. Allow the mimes to continue for a short time and then stop the action. Again, you could ask groups to show their mimes, time permitting.

Finally, ask the children to work in groups to mime the courtier's response to Firsten's trick and then to mime the princess's reaction to Firsten's trick.

STAGE 3:

Explain to the children that now they are going to put the freezes, the movements for the chorus and their group mimes all together while you read the three verses of the poem. They must listen very carefully for the cues you give them.

Ask the children to find a space and to gather into their original small groups of six to ten, and nominate a child in each of them to represent Firsten Last for verses 8 to 10 and a different child for the princess in verses 9 and 10.

Tell the children to begin with their freeze of the courtiers reacting to Firsten's arrival at the court and then instruct them to bring their freezes to life with mimed actions when they hear you say, 'Though I'll do nothing grand...'

Advise the children that as soon as they have completed their mimes of courtiers reacting to Firsten they should move into their smaller groups to perform the chorus.

Finally, they should move back into their original groups again to

Scholastic
DRAMA
Workshop

create the freeze of Firsten performing his trick while the courtiers watch, and then bring the freeze to life with mimed action when they hear you say, 'The princess looked… She saw…'

Instruct the children to freeze all action at the end of the poem, with the princess and Firsten and all the courtiers smiling broadly.

Ensure that children understand your instructions and are clear about what is expected of them, then ask them to position themselves in their starting freezes and slowly read through verses 8, 9 and 10 while they perform the accompanying mimes, movements and freezes.

If you think there are too many instructions for the children to absorb all at once, break the elements down and perform each verse individually first as a practice run, explaining before starting each one exactly what you want the children to do. Then repeat the whole process, without explanation, and running all three verses together to reinforce their responses.

Once the three verses have all been performed, thank the children for their work, praise their efforts and ask them to sit in a circle with you again. Initiate a brief recap discussion about the work they have achieved during the sessions so far and the processes they have used to bring the poem to life. Inform them that during the next – and final – session, you will ask them to bring all of these elements together to perform the whole poem. Praise their efforts again and ensure that they understand that the session has now ended.

FOLLOW-UP ACTIVITIES:
Ask the children to:
- improvise a discussion in pairs about what makes them smile or cheers them up
- draw a picture of each of the freezes they created (as in previous sessions).
- write captions for their drawings of the 'frozen' images (as in previous sessions).

PREPARATION FOR ACTIVITY SESSION 5:

Plan the groups for the performances of each verse in advance – it is too difficult and time-consuming to try to group children while the activity session is in progress. It will also ensure that you achieve positive group dynamics.

Have two or three options for the children who will play the princess and Firsten Last, just in case your original choices are absent. The princess does not have to be female and Firsten need not be male!

5

THE COMPLETE POEM

OBJECTIVES:

To consolidate all skills and knowledge through final performance, creating an overview of the poem.

RESOURCES:

School hall; photocopiable pages 101–106; 'role-on-the-wall' from previous session; grouping plans; paper; writing and drawing materials.

GROUP SIZE:

Whole group, small groups and individual work.

STAGE 1:

Sit in a circle with the children, hand out copies of the poem (photocopiable pages 101–105) and read it through while they follow. Explain that they will be bringing the whole poem to life, using all the methods they have experienced during previous sessions. Initiate a brief recap discussion, asking the children to relate the story contained in the poem and the methods they have applied in bringing that story to life.

Tell the children that you will create small groups which will each perform one verse of the poem, that one child will play the role of the princess throughout and that one child will play Firsten for the final three verses. Explain that the whole group, excluding the child playing the princess, will perform the chorus.

At this point allow the children to ask questions, and reinforce and clarify your instructions, or they will ask later in the session, which will slow the activities down.

Nominate the children you have chosen to play the princess and Firsten. Separate the class into groups to perform

On the 14th day of July

At the break of dawn

The competition to make the princess smile shall begin.

the poem. Children should be allowed to form their own groups for the movements for the chorus.

Follow this structure for the performance:

Verse 1: a group of six to ten children plus the princess to perform the freeze and mime of the king and courtiers reacting to the princess's activities.

Verse 2: the nursemaid commenting on the royal baby, and the king banishing all the mirrors in the palace.

Verse 3: pairs to perform the freeze and mime of the king's question and the princess's answer, groups of six to eight children being the townspeople, with one person being the town crier announcing the contest.

Verse 4: everyone in groups being the young men trying out their tricks for the smiling contest.

Verse 5: everyone in pairs to perform the freeze of the king and queen at prayer.

Verse 6: groups of six to eight children to perform the mime of the contestants trying to make the princess smile.

Verse 7: everyone in pairs to perform the movements of Nincom and Poop at the contest.

Verse 8: a group of six to ten children plus Firsten to perform the freeze and mime of the courtiers reacting to his arrival at the contest.

Verse 9: everyone to form smaller groups of four to six, excluding the princess, to perform the freeze as they wait for Firsten to perform his trick, while Firsten steps into the ring.

Verse 10: the princess reacting to Firsten's trick.

Final chorus: everyone together, including the princess and Firsten, smiling as they perform the movements.

STAGE 2:

Assign the children to their relevant groups and allocate verses to each group, then rehearse the performance by asking each group – and the children playing the princess and Firsten – to find a space in the hall to perform their freezes and mimes as they have done in previous sessions.

Do not use or read the poem at this point; this rehearsal should be an exercise in understanding the sequence of the process and should simply provide an opportunity to clarify what the children are required to do. The children should be familiar enough with the poem now to be able to recall exactly what happens in each verse and the freezes and mimes they need to create and perform. If any are unsure, use the opportunity to ask if any other children can remember – allowing an opportunity for specific input.

Work through each verse slowly, creating the freezes, bringing them to life with mime and grouping the children to perform the chorus. Repeat this process of rehearsal as many times as you feel necessary, until everyone is ready to perform to the poem.

STAGE 3:
Once you feel that the children are ready to perform to the poem being read aloud, ask them to return to their spaces in their groups and tell them that they will now perform the poem as you read it, listening carefully to the words. Ensure that the first group is ready and in position in their first freeze and then read through the poem slowly while the children respond with their freezes, mimes and movements.

Try to strike a reasonable balance between reading slowly enough for the children to respond but not reading so slowly that the pace becomes sluggish and boring. The children may want to repeat the performance, especially if things went wrong – if you have time, allow them to do that.

Whatever the outcome, praise the children for their concentration and effort and then gather them into a circle with you again.

Referring to the 'role-on-the-wall', ask the children if they want you to add or change anything about the princess on it, and respond to their suggestions, writing with a different coloured marker pen.

Conclude the session with a final discussion about the activities they have experienced during the project, asking questions such as: *Have you enjoyed learning about the princess? What did you enjoy the most? What did we learn from the story in the poem? Who are the other people in the story? How do you think the princess feels at the end of the story? What do you think happens next in the story?* And so on.

After this discussion, ask the children again if they would like to add or change anything on the role-on-the-wall, and respond to their comments and suggestions. Finally, thank them for their hard work and excellent performances and ensure that they understand that the project is now at an end.

FOLLOW-UP ACTIVITIES:
Ask the children to:
- write a story entitled 'The Princess Who Wouldn't Smile' – this can reflect events in the poem or be a completely original piece of work
- write a story about an impolite princess
- use the storyboard (photocopiable page 106) to draw pictures telling the story in the poem
- write captions underneath each drawing of the story
- draw a picture of the princess and Firsten at the end of the poem
- write or draw the story of 'what happens next', using captions if they draw pictures.

Scholastic
DRAMA
Workshop

Verse 1

The princess of a distant land was pale of face and sleek of hand,
She danced, she sang, she played the spoons, and – with her red lips – whistled tunes.
The only thing she didn't do was SMILE, and now, at twenty-two,
The time for marriage was well nigh. The king let out a king-sized sigh.

Oh dearest princess we would be glad
To see you smile and not look sad!

Verse 2

For never a smile did the princess show since the day she was born – when these words did flow:
"Isn't she ugly, the poor wee thing?" a nursemaid spoke cruelly of the royal offspring.
To protect his daughter, the king, in a fury, announced that all mirrors henceforth he would bury.
"I'll not have her thinking when spying her face that she's lacking in beauty and style and grace."

Oh dearest princess we would be glad
To see you smile and not look sad!

Verse 3

So the king sighed deeply, "What can we do to get someone to marry you?"
The princess thought, and after a while said, "I'll marry the man who makes me smile."
The town crier rode throughout the land, announcing the contest for the princess's hand.
Posters displayed the date and the time. The king was hopeful for a man in his prime.

Oh dearest princess we would be glad
To see you smile and not look sad!

Verse 4

Young men of the land rehearsed funny faces, telling bad jokes, holding three-legged races,
Some juggled, some tumbled and some played the clown. Others tried card tricks or hung upside down.
For just one smile would make some lucky chappy rich, renowned and royally happy!
And just one smile was what was required to give the king all he desired!

Oh dearest princess we would be glad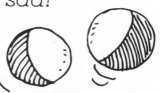
To see you smile and not look sad!

Verse 5

On the eve of the smiling contest day, the king and queen knelt down to pray:
"Dear God, please help us in our quest to do for our daughter what's right and best.
To see our daughter have some fun, we'd happily become like everyone.
To see her smile with mirth and pleasure, we'd gladly give up all our treasure!"

Oh dearest princess we would be glad
To see you smile and not look sad!

Verse 6

The contest lasted all day long, beginning at the break of dawn.
Ten seconds was the allotted time for games or jokes, tricks or rhymes.
Everyone tried their very best only to hear the judge shout, "Next!"
So even after the longest while, still the princess WOULD NOT SMILE.

Oh dearest princess we would be glad
To see you smile and not look sad!

Verse 7

The supply of suitors almost drained, only two more chaps remained.

First there was Nincom, then there was Poop. Nincom pulled his whole face through a hoop!

No smile… So Poop ate flaming swords, while tying himself in rubber cords!

Still no smile… But, wait… Who was this fellow dressed in white and gold and yellow?

Oh dearest princess we would be glad
To see you smile and not look sad!

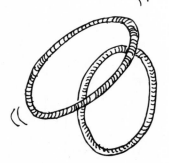

Verse 8

With bow and arrow, he stood so simple, laughing-eyed and cheeks a-dimple.

His name was strangely 'Firsten Last' and he said he'd come from the distant past.

Said he, "Though I'll do nothing grand, I'll make her smile, just with my hand.

Don't worry, King, you'll hear her laughter, from this day forth and ever after."

Oh dearest princess we would be glad
To see you smile and not look sad!

Scholastic
DRAMA
Workshop

Verse 9

As Firsten stepped into the ring, the solemn princess began to sing
The same soft song she'd sung all day: "Oh, make me smile and with you I'll stay!"
Said he, "Look at this silver mirror to see your own face, bright and clear!"
All lips fell silent and all cheeks paled – would Firsten win where the rest had failed?

Oh dearest princess we would be glad
To see you smile and not look sad!

Verse 10

The princess looked… She saw… She SMILED! Not for a minute, not for a while,
But on and on, her whole life long – at Firsten Last, and at everyone!
Firsten Last was the man she picked. Reflecting her own face did the trick!
So married they were, the smiling pair, bringing happiness to sad folk everywhere.

Oh dearest princess we are so glad
To see you smile and not look sad!

Clive Riche

STORYBOARD

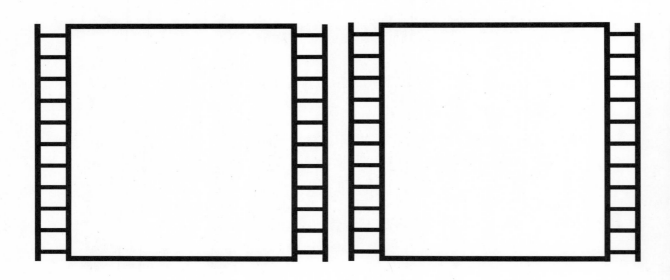

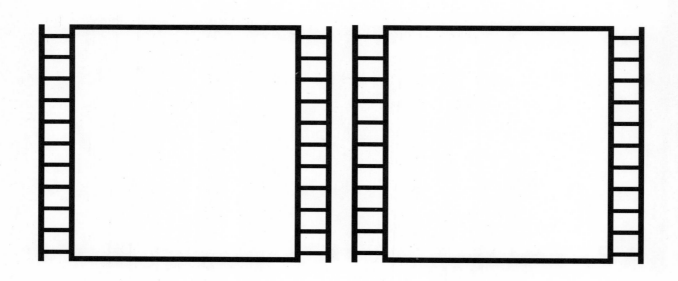

Scholastic **DRAMA** Workshop

Chapter Seven

CINDERELLA

INTRODUCTION

Project description

This is a short project based upon the familiar story of Cinderella. Simple drama methods are used to bring the story to life, exploring events, the story structure and characters. Through these methods, children are encouraged to approach this familiar text in a more analytical and reflective manner.

Why this project

This project enables teachers and children to understand the concept of text analysis in its most basic form, appreciating that the methods used for this analysis can be applied to any text. Children are encouraged to understand that texts contain more information than is often first perceived, and this understanding is increased through the development of their skills and the depth of their responses as the project progresses.

Length of project

Each activity session in this project, including the introductory session, is designed to be completed within 45 to 60 minutes. There are a total of four sessions, resulting in the complete project lasting approximately four hours, excluding any follow-on tasks. This could be completed over a period of half a term or during one intensive week.

Project organization

The project is organized into the following sections:

- introductory session – establishes the subject context
- activity session 1 – 'Simple storytelling'
- activity session 2 – 'Text improvisation'
- activity session 3 – 'Exploring characters in the text'
- photocopiable resource pages providing the story.

Learning aims

- Subject knowledge and understanding: (English) explores basic text analysis; (drama) introduces concept of characterization and role-play.
- Personal and social development: encourages analytical thought and appropriate responses; develops speaking and listening skills; builds confidence and stimulates whole-group approach.
- Creative development: encourages imaginative participation.

Drama strategies

The project provides opportunities for whole group, small group, pair and individual work and builds confidence slowly through these various approaches. Drama skills are developed progressively, from groups creating freezes, mimes and performing improvisations to more individual participation through characterization and role-play. Many of the drama conventions utilized are in simple form, enabling the children to develop their skills and understanding at a gentle pace. Teachers will be expected to respond in role as various characters when they are 'hot-seated' during activity session 3.

Resources needed

Photocopiable pages 117–122, school hall, chairs, flip chart or board, large space on classroom display board, A3 sheet of paper, A4 paper, writing and drawing materials.

What the children do

Children respond to questions which guide their exploration of a familiar text. They will be expected to consider their responses,

Scholastic
DRAMA
Workshop

reflecting, analysing and amending wherever required. Although the text is a familiar one, children will be required to discard any preconceptions and propose ideas which are original in their creativity. Children will be asked to respond as themselves during discussions and in role as characters from the text during the drama.

What the teacher does

The teacher will lead the discussions and guide the children in their conception of the dramatic context. Teachers should, wherever possible, enable the children to feel a strong sense of ownership about their work and should facilitate their creation of original ideas. The teacher is working out of role for much of the project, with the opportunity for being 'hot-seated' as various characters during activity session 3.

The most important aspect of the teacher's involvement is to encourage a feeling within the children that their contributions are valued and, thus, to build their confidence in responding to the creative process.

Assessment

Follow-on tasks contained within this project will assist in the assessment of knowledge gained. Creative writing tasks will assess understanding of the text. Use the assessment section of this book for recording achievements (see pages 13–20). Link assessment to the *Desirable Outcomes for Children's Learning* or KS1 level indicators.

INTRODUCTORY SESSION

Resources needed

Photocopiable pages 117–122, paper, board or flip chart, large space on classroom display board, writing and drawing materials.

What to do

Ask the children to sit in their classroom places, or sit with them in the reading corner. Hand out copies of the story of Cinderella (photocopiable pages 117–122) and read the story to them while they follow the text. Tell the children that they are going to use the story to do some drama work, but first they must make sure that they all understand exactly what happens in the story.

Explain to the children that they are going to help you to write the story outline on the board. Begin this process by asking the children: *How does the story start?* Sum up their responses with a simple observation such as 'A girl called Ella lived alone with her father because her mother had died'.

Encourage the children to be specific and economic in their use of language. Ensure that they understand that they are to provide short sentence responses, and ask them to think carefully about what happened next. After each contribution ask the children: *Is that right? Have we missed out anything important?* Once the whole group have agreed on the sentence, write it up on the board. Then continue in the same manner, gradually building up a series of sequential sentences which clarify events.

Ask the children to form pairs or small groups, and distribute drawing paper, crayons and writing implements. Allocate a sentence from the sequential notes to each pair or group and ask them to draw a picture to show what is happening in that sentence. Whether you choose small groups, pairs or possibly even individuals will depend on how many sentences you have which outline the story. Some children will go into great detail, highlighting every little aspect of the story, others will give brief notes which emphasize only what they consider to be the 'important' elements of the text.

Once the children have drawn their pictures representing their sentences, ask them to write the sentence underneath their picture, to provide a caption.

Thank the children for their work, collect in all of the drawings and mount them on the display board, in sequential order.

While you are creating the display, distribute more drawing paper and ask the children to draw a picture of Cinderella as they imagine her to look. This may result in some stereotypical pictures, but you might be surprised by some of the interpretations!

Inform the children that their story outline will be used for their drama in the next session. Praise them for their efforts and ensure that they understand that the session is now ended.

Preparation for activity session 1:

Write the story outline down as a series of sequential notes to retain as a basis for the drama work.

1

SIMPLE STORYTELLING

OBJECTIVES:

To consolidate textual knowledge by representing the devised story outline in actions.

RESOURCES:

School hall, story outline notes from introductory session.

GROUP SIZE:

Whole group and small group work.

STAGE 1:

Sit in a circle with the children and say: *Let's remind ourselves about what we did last time. Who can remember the work we did about Cinderella?* Allow various children to contribute until you are sure that you have recapped thoroughly and they are clear about the story outline which they completed.

Tell the children: *Today we are going to show the story of Cinderella, using the story notes that you made in the last lesson.* Ask them to form small groups of four to six and to find a space in the hall to work in.

If the children are too young to form their own groups, nominate the groupings yourself. In this first instance it is advisable to match children of similar abilities, as their confidence will be increased through the productivity of working with those who motivate them.

Inform the children that you are going to ask them to make 'frozen' pictures in their groups showing each of the sentences which tell the story of Cinderella. Advise them that you will read out each story outline sentence which they created during the previous session and then will allow them a few moments to prepare their picture. After that you will give everyone a countdown from five and then ask all of the groups to 'freeze' as if they were a photograph of that part of the story.

Emphasize to the children that when you give the 'freeze' command they must hold their positions as still as possible and in complete silence. Any children deliberately failing to do this should be quietly asked to sit aside until they feel able to participate sensibly.

Once you are sure that the children understand what is expected of them, work through the sequential notes in order, asking the children to create a freeze which represents each aspect of the story.

Children will take a few moments to grasp what is required of them, and a little while longer to respond to your instructions. However, you should gradually reduce the amount of time you allow for preparation as this will motivate them into thinking quickly and negotiating their roles more speedily. Praise all efforts – even those groups who do not manage to complete their full picture by the time you command them to 'freeze' – as this will ensure that they are motivated to try even harder

Scholastic
DRAMA
Workshop

next time. When all of the groups have completed a freeze representing each of the sentences, thank the children for their efforts and ask them to sit in a circle with you again.

STAGE 2:

Inform the children that you now want them to tell some parts of the story by using movements and actions only instead of 'frozen' pictures. Emphasize that this requires showing what happens in each part of the story using movements only and no words, noises or sounds and tell them that it is called mime.

Ask the children to form the same groups as before and to find a space to work in. Advise them that you will read each sentence out and then allow them a little time to plan and prepare before asking the groups to perform their mimes, in unison. (If you have time, you could ask some of the groups to show their mimes to the others, at this stage of the session.)

Choose specific aspects of the story for the children to perform in mime. These should include:
- the ugly sisters mistreating Cinderella
- the invitation to the ball arriving
- Cinderella with her fairy godmother watching the transformations
- at the ball
- the prince dancing with Cinderella
- the clock striking midnight, Cinderella leaving quickly and the prince finding Cinderella's lost shoe
- the ugly sisters trying on the shoe and the shoe fitting Cinderella
- the prince and Cinderella getting married.

When each group has performed each mimed section of the story together, advise the children that you are now going to give each group a different part of the story to mime in turn so that the whole class will tell the story of Cinderella, bit by bit.

You will have between four and eight groups, depending on the number of children in each group. This means that either you will have to reduce the storyline further, condensing it into fewer mimes, or that groups will have to perform two mimes.

STAGE 3:

Allocate to each group one or two specific aspects of the story, from either your own notes or the list above, ensuring that they are clear about what is expected of them and that they understand which mimes they have been requested to perform.

Allow between 5 and 10 minutes for preparation and rehearsal and then ask the groups to perform the mimes, to whatever stage they've reached, in sequential order while the other groups observe. Ensure that the 'audience' remains quiet and attentive while groups are performing their mimes.

Praise all efforts, thank the children for their contributions and ensure that the whole group are aware that the session is now at an end. Advise the children that they will be continuing with the story of Cinderella in the next session.

FOLLOW-UP ACTIVITIES:

Ask the children to:
- write about or draw the activities completed during the session
- write about or draw any scenes omitted which could have been included.

TEXT IMPROVISATION

OBJECTIVES:

To develop drama skills by bringing text to life through improvisation.

RESOURCES:

School hall, A3 sheet of paper, writing and drawing materials.

GROUP SIZE:

Whole group, small group, pair and individual participation within whole-group work.

STAGE 1:

Sit with the children in a circle. Initiate a whole-group discussion about activity session 1, asking the children: *What did we do about the story of Cinderella in the last lesson?* Allow time to acknowledge, and praise all contributions.

Tell the children that they are going to act out the story of Cinderella again, but this time using words and sounds as well as actions. Ask them to stand in a space in the hall and to listen carefully to your instructions. Advise them that in a moment you are going to ask them to walk about the room carefully without bumping into each other. Explain that while they are walking around, they will need to listen carefully for you clapping your hands together and that, when they hear this signal, they must stand still, in silence.

Inform the children that when they are all standing silently, you will call out a number, which will mean that they should then get into a group of that number of people. Advise them that when they have formed their group, you will give them one of the scenes from the story of Cinderella to act out in their groups. Advise them that they should start acting that scene out straight away, making up whatever they think the characters in that scene would say to each other and what they think they would do.

When the children have all understood your instructions and appreciate what is expected of them, ask them to walk around the room quietly and carefully. It is a good idea to ask children to look for empty floor space to walk into. This ensures that they concentrate more on where they are going, rather than who they are with. However, children will often try to move around the room in packs with their friends and you should actively discourage this.

STAGE 2:

Each improvisation which you ask the children to perform must be based on a different section of the story and contain a varying number of characters. Scenes and groupings should include the following:

- the ugly sisters and stepmother ordering Cinderella about (four children)
- the invitation to the ball arriving (five children – characters as above, plus Cinderella's father)
- Cinderella being transformed by her fairy godmother (two children)
- at the ball where the prince and Cinderella are dancing (eight children)

- the clock striking twelve, Cinderella leaving and the prince finding her shoe (eight children)
- the ugly sisters trying on the shoe and the shoe fitting Cinderella (four children)
- the prince and Cinderella getting married (ten children).

After the children have walked around the room for a short while, and once you feel that they are all listening for your signal, clap your hands. When they are all quietly listening, ask them to form a group of the appropriate number of children and make your instructions specific, for example saying: *I want you to imagine that you are Cinderella's stepmother and two stepsisters ordering Cinderella about and asking her to do lots of jobs for you. You must decide very quickly who you all are and then pretend to be that person, saying and doing exactly what they would say and do. All right? Off you go.*

Allow each improvisation to continue for a few moments and then clap your hands again, to signal to the children that they should stand still, in silence. Praise all efforts then ask the children to walk around the room on their own again before clapping your hands once more and repeating the instructions with a different scene. Continue with this process until all of the scenes have been improvised.

Thank the children for their work and then ask them to sit in a circle with you again, bringing with you a sheet of A3 paper and some marker pens.

STAGE 3:

Ask the children: *Who are the different characters in the story of Cinderella? Can you tell me the names of the people in the story?* As the children make their suggestions, write the names of the characters clearly on the A3 sheet, acknowledging all responses. This exercise should result in a list which includes the following:

- Cinderella (or 'Ella')
- Cinderella's father
- Cinderella's stepmother
- ugly sister/stepsister 1
- ugly sister/stepsister 2
- fairy godmother
- the prince
- possibly – the king.

Encourage the children to consider any additional characters who appeared in the story of Cinderella that you read to them by saying: *Is there anyone important who is in the story that we have missed out?* When you are sure that all possible characters have been noted, thank the children for their contributions.

Distribute some drawing paper and crayons and instruct the children to draw a picture of one of the characters from the list you have compiled. Ensure that this exercise results in a drawing of every character by allocating 'spare' characters to those children who can't make up their mind who to draw, or to children who complete their initial drawings quickly while others are still working.

Collect in the drawings, thank the children for their work and advise them that this session is now ended. Tell them that they will be working on the story of Cinderella again in the next session, thinking especially about the different people in the story.

When you return to the classroom, mount the children's drawings onto the display board alongside the other 'Cinderella' work.

FOLLOW-UP ACTIVITIES:
Ask the children to:
- draw a picture of another character from the story
- write a description of the character they drew during the session
- document the activity session in drawings or writing
- write one of their improvisations out in scripted form
- give each unnamed character a 'proper' name – this could be completed as a whole-group exercise.

EXPLORING CHARACTERS IN THE TEXT

OBJECTIVES:
To provide an opportunity for basic character analysis.

RESOURCES:
School hall, A3 sheet of character names from previous session, chair, photocopiable pages 117–122.

GROUP SIZE:
Whole group and individual participation within whole-group context.

STAGE 1:
Sit with the children in a circle. Initiate a discussion about the previous session, asking them: *Who can remember what work we did on Cinderella in the last lesson?* Acknowledge and confirm all responses. Inform the children that today their drama will be about the characters in the story of Cinderella, and ask: *Who can tell me the names of the people in the story that we wrote down in the last lesson?* Again, acknowledge and confirm responses, using the A3 sheet of character names as a reference point.

Tell the children: *First I am going to ask you to think about how these different people move and how they might walk about.* Lead a brief discussion about how each character might walk, for example by asking such questions as: *How would Cinderella move? Would she walk quickly or slowly? Would it be a sad or a happy walk? What does a sad walk look like?* When you have discussed possible modes of movement for each of the characters on your A3 list, ask the children to stand in a space in the hall and to listen carefully.

Tell them that you are going to ask them to walk around the room in the style of each of the characters and that they must listen for your signal of a hand clap, when you will give them a different character name.

Begin by asking them to start walking around the room as the character of Cinderella, and then continue with the other characters, working through your list, clapping your hands each time to change their movements to a different character. When all the children have walked about as each of the characters, praise all their efforts, thank them for their work and then ask them to sit in a circle with you again.

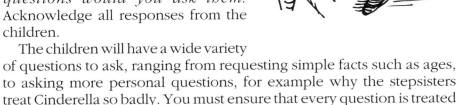

STAGE 2:

Bring your 'hot-seating' chair forward and sit on it in front of the children. Initiate a brief discussion about the way the characters in the story behave, saying: *It would be interesting to ask some of the people in this story questions, wouldn't it? What characters would you like to talk to if you could and what questions would you ask them?* Acknowledge all responses from the children.

The children will have a wide variety of questions to ask, ranging from requesting simple facts such as ages, to asking more personal questions, for example why the stepsisters treat Cinderella so badly. You must ensure that every question is treated with the same respect and that all are responded to positively.

Inform the children that you are now going to pretend to be one of the characters from the story. Ask them: *Who would you like to speak to first?* When they respond, tell them that they must now imagine that you are that person. Go into role using your body language and, when appropriate, your voice, and say: *I am (whichever character it is). What would you like to know?* The children may be hesitant at first, but gentle encouragement will prompt a flood of questions. Try to ensure that they don't all speak at once but raise their hands when they want to ask a question.

Come out of role by saying: *Well, that was interesting, wasn't it? Who would you like to speak to now?* Repeat this process of going in and out of role with several characters, until all the possibilities for productive questioning have been exhausted.

Thank the children for their interesting questions and conclude with a brief discussion about any new facts or interesting issues that the hot-seating session may have raised.

STAGE 3:

Tell the children that you are now going to ask them to devise a silent action which represents each of the characters mentioned in the story. Explore what actions could physically represent each character by asking: *What action could we do to show the character of Cinderella? What action would make you think of Cinderella?*

Using this method of questioning, devise a short and simple action to represent each of the characters mentioned in the story. Base the actions on knowledge of the characters gained during the hot-seating session in stage 2. The actions should be easy to perform and must be able to be repeated a number of times. Rehearse each of the actions for all of the characters two or three times until the children are completely familiar with each one. These character actions could include:

- Cinderella cleaning
- Cinderella's father writing letters or working
- the ugly sisters putting on make-up or combing their hair
- Cinderella's stepmother filing her nails
- the fairy godmother performing magic
- the prince shaking the imaginary hands of his adoring public.

Now test the children's memory and responses by making this into a quick game: call out the name of a character at random – can they perform the action for that character without hesitation?

When you are sure that all of the children are conversant with each character action, explain that you will now read the story of Cinderella again and that they should perform their agreed action for each character every time that character's name is mentioned in the story.

Once you are sure that the children understand what is expected of them, ask them to stand in a space in the hall and advise them to listen carefully as you read the story (photocopiable pages 117–122) and to respond with their actions immediately that they hear a character's name mentioned.

Read through the story slowly, allowing the children time to acknowledge all of the different characters mentioned. Some of the changes from one action to another are very quick, and may cause laughter and a drop in concentration. This is acceptable but do not continue reading until all of the children are listening attentively again. The exercise will take some time, but children will be completely focused during it as they listen carefully for the names of the characters and perform the corresponding actions. Some children will take longer to respond than others, but working at a different pace is also acceptable.

When you have finished reading the story, thank and praise the children for their efforts and ask them to sit in a circle with you again. Lead a brief final discussion about any additional facts or knowledge the children might have gained about the story through working on this project. As a starting point, ask them: *What do you know now about Cinderella's story that you didn't know before?* Acknowledge all responses, thank the children for their work and ensure that they understand that the project is now at an end.

FOLLOW-UP ACTIVITIES:
- Create a 'role-on-the-wall' for one or all of the characters to build character knowledge (see page 32 in the glossary).

Ask the children to:
- draw or write a description of one of the characters using any new information to add further detail
- document the activity session in drawings or writing.

As a class:
- Repeat the same process with a different story.

Scholastic
DRAMA
Workshop

There was once a girl called Ella whose mother had died. For a long time she lived alone with her father, but he was very unhappy and lonely, and he eventually decided to remarry. His new wife was also a widow and brought with her to the house her two daughters from her first marriage.

These two daughters took an instant dislike to their new sister. They shouted at Ella and bossed her around, making her do all the work and not treating her like a sister at all.

Even when she'd finished her jobs, Ella wasn't invited to join the rest of the family. Instead she had to spend her evenings in the kitchen, getting dusty and dirty from raking the dying cinders in the fire to try and keep warm. The stepsisters used to mock her and call her 'Cinders Ella', and eventually the name stuck and Ella became known as Cinderella.

One day the stepsisters and their mother received an invitation to a ball at the palace. They were thrilled and so excited. Everyone knew that the prince had been instructed by his father, the king, to find a wife. Perhaps he would choose one of the ladies at the ball as his bride!

The two sisters immediately began to try to make themselves as beautiful as possible, in the hope of catching the prince's eye. They bought the most expensive dresses, the most elaborate jewellery and had their hair styled in the most exotic way. However, all of their efforts made very little difference as, unlike Cinderella, the stepsisters were not naturally beautiful!

The evening of the ball finally arrived and, as her stepsisters drove off in their carriage, Cinderella sat in the kitchen in her usual place next to the fire, quietly crying to herself.

"What's the matter, Cinderella?" a gentle voice asked.

Cinderella sobbed, "I wish I could go to the ball myself."

"And so you shall," the voice said.

Cinderella looked up, startled and a little bit afraid. A beautiful lady was standing beside her.

"Do not be afraid, sweet Cinderella," the beautiful lady said, "I am your fairy godmother, and I am here to see that your wish comes true."

Cinderella gasped with joy, amazed that someone could be so kind to her.

The beautiful fairy godmother smiled again at Cinderella, and then became quite business-like.

"Now, Cinderella, we have no time to waste if you are going to make it to the ball! Fetch me a pumpkin."

Cinderella looked puzzled, but did as she was told. The fairy godmother touched the pumpkin with her magic wand, and it suddenly turned into a wonderful golden coach.

"Now find me six mice…"

Cinderella fetched them as quickly as possible, and her fairy godmother touched them again with her magic wand, turning them into beautiful horses to pull the coach.

"Now fetch me a rat please…"

Upon Cinderella's return with a large brown rat, the fairy godmother used her magic to turn it into a coachman in a golden-braided uniform.

"And six lizards please…"

The fairy godmother turned them into splendidly dressed footmen to run behind the coach.

When the magic had been completed, the fairy godmother turned to Cinderella with a smile. With one final touch of her magic wand, the rags Cinderella had been wearing became a dress so magnificent and beautiful that it took your breath away. In Cinderella's wonderful golden hair sparkled tiny jewels and on her feet glittered a pair of delicate glass slippers. Cinderella threw her arms around the fairy godmother and thanked her over and over again for the wonderful transformation.

"It is unnecessary to thank me, Cinderella," the fairy godmother said, "just make sure that you have a marvellous time at the ball."

"I will," said Cinderella happily, "oh, I will."

"I must give you one word of warning, though," the fairy godmother continued. "You must be home by midnight – for on the final stroke of twelve o'clock your dress will turn back to rags, your coach to a pumpkin, your horses to mice and everything will be just as before. If you do not leave before the final stroke of midnight, everyone will see your transformation back into poor little Cinderella. Please remember what I say. Now, off you go and enjoy yourself."

That night Cinderella was the belle of the ball. Everyone wondered who she was. They all thought that maybe she was a princess from a faraway land. All of the ladies, including her two stepsisters, admired her beautiful dress and begged her for the name of her dressmaker. The gentlemen all wanted to kiss her hand and dance with her.

Eventually the prince asked her to dance with him and, stunned by her beauty and gentle nature, he

Scholastic
DRAMA
Workshop

fell in love with her at first sight. No one else was able to dance with Cinderella after that. The minutes whirled away and Cinderella had the most wonderful evening of her life.

Suddenly the clock began to strike twelve and Cinderella remembered the words of her fairy godmother. She was terrified that the prince and all the people at the ball would see her become poor, raggedy Cinderella again. So, without even a final goodbye, she picked up her dress and ran as fast as she could out of the palace and away from the ball.

"Come back!" the prince called, but Cinderella carried on running, tripping on the palace steps in her haste to be away and losing one of her delicate glass slippers as she did so. With no time to stop and pick it up, she left it where it lay and continued running home. By the time she reached the street, her dress was rags again.

That night, back in her usual place by the fire in the kitchen, Cinderella cried herself to sleep. She knew that life would never be so marvellous again.

But that wasn't true. As he ran after her, the prince found Cinderella's slipper on the palace steps. He knew that the delicate glass shoe belonged to the woman he wanted to marry. So the next morning, the prince went all around the town from house to house, asking every lady to try the slipper on.

"If I don't find the beautiful stranger who wore it last night, I shall be unhappy forever and will never marry at all," he said.

The slipper did not fit any of the feet offered to the prince. He was beginning to resign himself to a life alone when, at last, he reached Cinderella's house. The two stepsisters were eager to prove to the prince that they were his intended bride! They pushed and pulled and squeezed and tried to make the glass slipper fit. But it was no use, their feet were just too big and too wide.

Broken-hearted, for this was the last house left for him to try, the prince was about to leave when he noticed what he thought was a poor servant girl, dusty and dirty from raking the fire cinders.

"Madam," he said gallantly, but without much hope, "why don't you try the slipper on too?"

"Her? Don't be silly!" the stepsisters cried together. "She didn't go to the ball, she was at home in her rightful place by the kitchen fire!"

But the prince insisted. He could see, underneath the dirt, how beautiful Cinderella was. The stepsisters held their breath as the prince placed the slipper on Cinderella's foot and, of course, it fitted her perfectly. Spitting with rage and jealousy, the two sisters could only look on as, realizing with joy that he had found his beautiful stranger again, the prince knelt and asked Cinderella to marry him.

And Cinderella happily said yes!

Scholastic
DRAMA
Workshop

Scholastic
WORKSHOP

Chapter Eight

THE ZOO
COMPANY

INTRODUCTION

Project description

This project provides links to the National Curriculum requirements on 'Life processes and living things'. It is based on the concept of children working in role as the staff of a zoo, with the teacher as the facilitator in role as the zoo director. Once the zoo arena has been established, additional drama contexts enable the children to explore and experience a variety of issues concerned with the creation and running of a zoo.

Why this project?

This project provides young children with an introduction to understanding animals, their natural habitat, diet, care requirements and the responsibilities associated with looking after them. The initial stages of the project require children to research and exchange information about the different types of animals which can be found in a zoo setting. The project sessions allow for a developmental progression in their individual participation, beginning with a whole-group approach and leading to more individual involvement. Various drama conventions are used, from whole-group discussion to telephone conversations, enabling children to learn through experiential involvement.

Length of project

Each activity session in the project, including the introductory session, is designed to be completed within 45 to 60 minutes. There are a total of six sessions, including the introductory session, resulting in the complete project being approximately six hours long. This could be delivered through one session per week during a term or completed in one intensive week of work.

Project organization

The project is organized into the following sections:

- introductory session – introduces and explores the subject context
- activity session 1 – 'Paper location – creating the zoo plan'
- activity session 2 – 'Working in the zoo – establishing roles in context'
- additional activity sessions providing optional drama contexts which expand the original concept and enable children to explore other issues (these are categorized under the following titles: 'The zoo company garden', 'The zoo company in trouble' and 'The zoo company wins a prize')
- photocopiable resources.

Learning aims

- Personal and social development: developing a sense of responsibility; finding solutions to problems.
- Communication skills: generates whole-group discussions; encourages children to use appropriate language, both formal and informal; prompts children to formulate appropriate questions and responses.
- Subject knowledge and understanding: (life processes) knowledge of animals and plants; (drama) provides opportunities to experience various conventions; (English) creative and structured writing opportunities; (art) animal drawings, devising and creating plans.

Drama strategies

Initial sessions build confidence by being centred upon a whole-group approach. The emphasis then moves on to small group involvement and, finally, individual participation within the group context. The drama conventions used in this project move from whole-group role-play, through small-group and individual role-play to more sophisticated responses, such as freezes, mime,

Scholastic
DRAMA
Workshop

telephone conversations, meetings and thought-tracking. It would be sensible to ensure that children were equipped for these drama conventions by providing one or two pre-project sessions using the discrete activities chapter of this book to introduce specific drama techniques. For example, 'Up, down freeze' (see page 40) and 'Freeze in role' (see page 64) introduces children to the concept of freezes; 'Animal families' (see page 56) and some of the movement exercises could be used to introduce the concept of mime and provide an introduction to the subject of animals.

Resources needed

Animal pictures in books – find ones of animals regularly found in a zoo; animal names written on pieces of paper; large sheet (A1 size at least) of paper for the zoo plan; Blu-Tack to help when planning the zoo (enables pieces of paper to be placed, lifted and moved as required); photocopies of your sketch of the final zoo plan; pieces of blank paper cut out to create zoo areas; pictures of trees, shrubs and flowers from books; written information on the trees, shrubs and flowers – that is, their environment, care requirements and so on to show to the children in order to aid their planning exercise; a play telephone; photocopiable pages 142–146; storyboard (photocopiable page 106); writing and drawing materials.

What the children do

Children establish and sustain roles as zookeepers and workers, undertaking various tasks at the zoo, from caring for the animals to working in the zoo shop or animal food store. They should be encouraged to remain in role throughout the project and to respond effectively to the drama contexts. Occasionally, during fact-finding sessions or discussions, children will be given the opportunity to step out of role and to participate as themselves, in order to aid their ability to research, reflect and analyse.

What the teacher does

Initial sessions require a structured teaching approach to ensure that children gather and process all the information required. Once the zoo context has been established, the teacher adopts and remains in role as the zoo director and continues to guide the project from within the context in that role.

During additional information-gathering sessions, the teacher may step out of role briefly to ensure that the children are 'on task'. The teacher's main purpose is that of facilitator and guide, leading the drama to achieve specific learning outcomes, while also ensuring that the children are empowered to direct the drama.

Assessment

Reinforce knowledge about animals by asking children to write a short passage about one of the zoo animals, noting their country of origin, natural habitats, eating habits, care requirements and so on.

Use the storyboard at the end of the project (see photocopiable page 106) for children to draw a sequenced picture series of the events they experienced during the project. Older children should also include short captions beneath each picture. Use the assessment section of this book for recording achievements (see pages 13–20). Link assessment to the *Desirable Outcomes for Children's Learning* or KS1 level indicators.

INTRODUCTORY SESSION

Resources needed

Large sheet of paper for display; display board; photocopiable page 142; animal information books with pictures; board or flip chart; paper; writing and drawing materials.

What to do

Ask the children to sit in a circle or in their classroom places where they can see you clearly. Show the children the animal pictures from the books and ask them to name them. Reveal a little information about each animal. Discuss the animals: considering which country they might come from, what type of environment they might live in, what foods they might eat, and so on. Explore through discussion how animals reveal information about themselves, for instance, giraffes have long necks which enable them to reach the leaves on tall trees; polar bears have thick coats which protect them in their icy environment, and so on.

Introduce the concept of zoos. Ask the children to suggest which animals live in zoos – encourage them to recall any zoo visits they may have made and to try and remember animals they have seen there. Discuss why zoos exist and how they can help the animals to survive. Ask the children: *Can we think of six or seven animals that live in a zoo?* Show them the pictures of these animals again, if you have them. Write on the board the animal names suggested, as a reference point. (You may receive suggestions for which you have no picture. This is perfectly acceptable.)

Ask the children to draw pictures of animals that live in a zoo. Ensure that each animal has a drawing by asking the children to indicate their choice of animal. Allow some children to copy animal pictures from the books if they wish.

While the children are drawing, write out the six or seven animal names they have specified on pieces of paper to use for the display.

When they have finished their drawings, put the children into small groups of three or four. Give each group a zoo animal to research. Ask them to read through the books and find information, or recall any facts you have imparted, and using the 'Zoo animal fact sheet' on photocopiable page 142, to write or draw five facts about their animal. These facts should include country of origin, preferred habitat, feeding habits, level of aggression (if relevant) and any other facts which you think may be essential knowledge.

While the children are researching their animals, collect their drawings and place them on the display board around the outside of a very large, blank sheet of paper. Group the animals together with the animal names you have written out.

Ask the groups to reveal what they have discovered about the different animals during their research. Refer to their pictures now placed on the display board. Reinforce the fact that the six or seven animals they have chosen can all be found in a zoo in this country. Tell the children that they are going to plan and create their own zoo, choosing where the animal areas are, what other animals they will have, if any, and what other areas and facilities will be in their zoo, and inform them that they are going to become zookeepers and zoo workers in their zoo. Tell the children that the large sheet of blank paper on the display board will become their zoo plan.

If you would like the children to carry out some further work at home, you could set them the task of doing more research about specific animals prior to the next session if you wish, although this is not strictly necessary.

Collect together all of the 'Zoo animal fact sheets' and display them prominently with the animal books for the children to use as an additional reference point.

Preparation for activity session 1

Rewrite the animal names on slips of paper for planning your zoo areas. Prepare blank paper shapes to plan additional zoo facilities.

Scholastic
DRAMA
Workshop

1

PAPER LOCATION – CREATING THE ZOO PLAN

OBJECTIVES:
To establish the creative setting for the drama.

RESOURCES:
Animal names rewritten on small slips of paper; large sheet of paper for zoo plan; blank paper shapes for planning zoo facilities; spare blank paper slips and shapes; Blu-Tack; writing and drawing materials.

GROUP SIZE:
Whole class and small groups.

STAGE 1:
Explain to the children that they are going to plan their zoo in detail. Gather the children around you at the display board, ensuring that they

can all see the board clearly. Use the display board as a reference point to recap what animals they decided lived in their zoo. Discuss with the children where the animal areas would be in their zoo and encourage them to make suggestions through asking them questions, for instance: *Which part of the zoo will be the crocodile area? Where shall we put the lions? What would be the best place for the penguins?*

Make the questions relevant to the animals they have chosen. Affix a small piece of Blu-Tack to the back of each of the animal names you have written out and use this to place, remove, move and replace the animal names on the large sheet of blank paper in the centre of your display board. Negotiate with the children until both you and they are happy with the positioning of all the animal areas in the zoo. Make sure you leave plenty of room to add other zoo facilities, such as the food store, shop, zoo director's office, garden and so on.

If you have only four or five animals, now is the time to use your spare slips of paper, in discussion with the children, to add more animals if necessary – and if you have the room on your zoo plan!

STAGE 2:
Tell the children that they are now going to design their animal areas in more detail, so that the animals can live happily in the zoo. Ask them to suggest what kinds of things they need to think about when planning the zoo areas for their animals to live in. Refer them back to the 'Zoo animal fact sheets' to consider habitat, natural environment, food requirements, care needs and so on.

Put the children into groups of three or four. Ask them to sit together in their groups at a table. Give each group a blank paper shape, some crayons or felt-tipped pens and allocate each group an animal name. This could be the same animal as they researched in the introductory session or a completely different one. Ask each group of children to work together to plan and design the 'living area' for their allocated animal. Instruct them to write their animal's name very clearly at the top of their plan.

Move around the classroom discussing the plans with the children. Ask them questions to focus their work, such as: *What does your animal eat? Does that mean you will need trees in your plan? Your animal lives in water – how are you going to provide it? Your animal is dangerous to humans – how can you make sure it doesn't escape? Where will your animal sleep? Your animal is really big – how are you going to make sure it has enough room to move about in?* and so on.

Allow the children a fixed period of time to complete their animal area plans – anything from 10 to 20 minutes, depending on their age and ability level. Then collect in the animal area plans and gather the children around you again at the display board, as previously. Show and discuss each plan as a whole group, checking with all the children that the areas have been designed to meet all the needs of each particular animal. Ask for suggestions of any aspects regarding care, habitat, food requirements and so on, which may have been omitted. Refer back to the research the children did on each of the animals to ensure that all requirements have been met and that plans are as complete and comprehensive as possible.

If the children manage to design comprehensive plans at their first attempt, excellent! If you feel that details still need to be added, ask them to get into their small groups again and to continue working on the designs for their animal areas until both you and they are satisfied with the results.

The plans should now look similar to the one represented in Figure 1. Gather together all the plans and replace the animal names on the main zoo plan with the children's designs of their animal areas.

Figure 1

STAGE 3:

Ask the children for suggestions of other facilities which they would like in their zoo. You may have to give them one of the examples from those suggested in the notes in stage 1 to start them off. Discuss what other facilities the zoo must have as an essential part of its overall plan. Use the blank, spare shapes of paper to write down the suggestions made by the children and, in negotiation with them, place them in appropriate locations on the main zoo plan.

If you have any spare time at this point, ask the children to get into

Scholastic
DRAMA
Workshop

their small groups again, and allocate each group one of these facilities to plan and design. Work through the same process as with the designing of the animal areas.

You should now have a complete zoo plan which resembles Figure 2 in its style of composition.

Figure 2

FOLLOW-UP ACTIVITIES:

Ask the children to:

- continue working on their designs for both animal areas and facilities as part of their general curriculum work
- write a diary of the work they have completed so far.

PREPARATION FOR ACTIVITY SESSION 2:

Save the animal names on the slips of paper which you removed from the zoo plan when replacing them with the children's designs of their animal areas – these will be used to represent zoo areas in the next lesson. Write out the additional facilities on blank pieces of paper – to be used for the same purpose. Create your own version of Figure 2 by drawing your complete zoo plan on A4 paper, to be used as a photocopiable resource later.

2

WORKING IN THE ZOO – ESTABLISHING ROLES IN CONTEXT

OBJECTIVES:

To create and develop roles within the drama context.

RESOURCES:

Zoo plan from previous session; slips of paper with animal names written on them; pieces of paper with additional zoo facilities on them; photocopiable page 143; Blu-Tack; writing materials.

GROUP SIZE:

Whole group, small groups and individual participation within whole-group context.

STAGE 1:

Briefly recap the activities from the previous session. Explain to the children that the classroom is now going to become the zoo. In negotiation with the children, establish where the zoo areas are in the classroom, referring to the zoo plan, and indicate these placements using the animal names and facilities which you have

written on pieces of paper. Use Blu-Tack to stick these pieces of paper indicating the animal areas and facilities in the designated areas of the classroom. Try not to take too long in deciding which areas of the classroom should represent which zoo areas. If you need more space, chairs should be moved out of the way or, where practicable, placed on tables.

Decide where your zoo entrance is – possibly the classroom door – and position the animal areas and facilities in relation to this. Divide the children into small groups. Ensure that you have enough groups to provide between one and four zoo workers for each animal area or facility. Allocate the children their designated areas and ask them to move to the corresponding areas in the classroom. You should now have a classroom separated into zoo areas for both animals and facilities, and between one and four children ready to work in each of their allocated zoo areas.

Some children may complain if they are given an area which they feel is 'uninteresting'. Be prepared for this and either use positive encouragement, for example by telling them that you thought they were very sensible and you need someone sensible to work in the food store, or by assuring them that you will have a very important task for them to do later. Then be sure to create one!

Tell the children that they are all now zoo workers and animal zookeepers and that you are now the zoo director, in charge of their zoo. Ask them what jobs they have to do in their different zoo areas, and make sure you respond positively to every contribution. Instruct the children to start working on their different jobs in their zoo areas by using the command: 'Right zoo workers, get on with your jobs please.' The children will respond to this and will start miming their various jobs, or will role-play with others and discuss the work they are doing. If some children stand silently, not responding but watching others, it would be best to leave them alone to observe. They will respond in their own time and when they feel confident. A little individual positive encouragement sometimes works, in the form of a quiet question, such as 'What jobs have you got to do today?'

STAGE 2:

Allow this activity to continue for a few moments and then give the children a signal that they are to stop work, either by raising your hand

Scholastic
DRAMA
Workshop

or saying, 'Excuse me zoo workers, could you stop working for a moment please?' or by using the 'Freeze' command, if the children are familiar with it. When all the activity has ceased and you are sure that the children are paying attention, instruct them that, as the zoo director, you need to check exactly what jobs they are going to do in their zoo areas.

Address each group, asking for individual or group responses to your question, for example, 'Lion keepers, what are you doing?' Continue this questioning around the group until everyone has responded with a specific task. This is to ensure that the activity now has a purpose and that children's roles are clearly defined.

Finish the questioning session with 'Thank you very much, zoo workers. Please carry on with your work now.' The children will return to miming or role-playing their various jobs, but should proceed with a much stronger sense of purpose. Allow this to continue for a few moments, moving around the room to ensure that the children remain on task.

Stop the activity using your chosen method from those mentioned above. Tell the children that, as zoo director, you are concerned to notice that they are not wearing the right clothes or uniforms for their jobs and that they don't seem to have the correct tools. Inform the children that they must all now put on their uniforms and gather their tools. This should be done as a whole group mime with you participating as well. Start the activity with: 'Right, everyone. Clothes first.' Then mime putting on your suit, hat, buttoning up your jacket and so on. The children should respond by miming putting on their own particular uniforms for their particular jobs. Repeat the process with them gathering the tools they will need: 'Now gather your tools together.' You could collect a watch, pen, clipboard, mobile phone, or whatever you feel a zoo director would use!

End this stage by saying, 'Good! Now that you all have the correct clothing and tools, could you please return to completing your jobs for today? Thank you.' The children should return to their various tasks. Remain in role as the zoo director and move around the room, keeping the children on task by asking them various questions about what they are doing, why they are doing it, what problems they are experiencing, if any, how their animals are, what job they are going to tackle next and why. Ensure that you praise and encourage all contributions, especially those zoo workers who are really working hard at their tasks.

Remain in role at all times. Children will often respond much more positively to you in role as the zoo director than as the teacher!

STAGE 3:
Allow the activity to continue for quite a while, ensuring that the

children remain in role as zoo workers throughout. Watch carefully for any children who seem to be losing interest, and ensure that you prompt them into working in role again by giving them specific tasks or asking specific questions. It is essential that the process of the children working in role as zookeepers and staff is closely monitored and guided by you at all times.

Stop the activity and tell the children that you are calling a meeting for them to report on the work they have done at the zoo during the day. If possible, sit the children in a circle, if not, ask them to sit on chairs in their zoo areas. Ask them to provide verbal reports of the jobs they completed. Allow all children the opportunity to respond, and encourage appropriate responses by asking them to be specific about their jobs and any problems they might have encountered.

Once this verbal reporting is completed, tell the children that zoo regulations insist that they complete written 'Daily report forms'. Distribute one of these forms (photocopiable page 143) to each zoo area and ask the children to complete it. Instruct them to discuss with each of their co-workers exactly what they all did during the day, noting any tasks they still have to complete, how the animals behaved, what they ate and so on, and to write these contributions down on the forms.

Allow the children a specific length of time to complete the daily report forms – 15 to 30 minutes, depending on the age and ability level of the children. Walk around the room, helping the children to remember by asking questions or giving prompts where necessary.

Still in role as zoo director, thank the zoo workers for their hard work and for completing the daily report forms and tell them that the zoo is now closed for the day.

File or store the daily report forms carefully and let the children observe you doing this, to show them that you acknowledge their contributions and take them seriously.

FOLLOW-UP ACTIVITIES:
Ask the children to:
- write a description of their allocated zoo area and the jobs they are responsible for
- draw their zoo area and include themselves doing specific jobs in that area.

PREPARATION FOR ACTIVITY SESSION 3:
Make a note of the zoo layout used in the classroom. Save the pieces of paper with the animal names and facilities on them to use in the next session. Photocopy enough copies of your drawn zoo plan to ensure one between two children. Collect pictures of trees, shrubs and flowers together with information for planning the zoo garden.

THE ZOO COMPANY GARDEN

OBJECTIVES:

To expand subject knowledge into the area of 'living things' by planning a zoo garden.

RESOURCES:

Pictures of trees, shrubs and flowers; photocopied drawn zoo plans; animal names and zoo facilities for re-creating zoo arena in the classroom; prompt sheet of classroom positions of different zoo areas (optional); completed daily report forms from previous session; photocopiable page 143 (blank 'Daily report forms'); writing and drawing materials.

GROUP SIZE:

Whole group, small groups and individual participation within whole-group context.

STAGE 1:

Advise the children that you are going to work in your zoo again and ask them to help you to re-create the zoo in the classroom, placing the animal names and facilities in the correct areas. Use a prompt sheet of classroom positions of zoo areas to assist you, if necessary. Ask the children to go to their work places and to put on their uniforms and gather their tools. Join them in this activity, using the mime to get into role as the zoo director.

Using the report forms completed by the children in the previous session, give them instructions regarding the jobs they have to do in their various zoo areas. Make these tasks quite specific. When all the children understand what is expected of them, allow them to continue working in the zoo for a short while, ensuring that they are all 'on task' and focused on their work.

Ask the children to stop working. Come out of role. Inform the children that in a moment you are going to ask them to continue working and that, after a short while, you will be instructing them to 'freeze' and will then ask them to explain exactly what they were doing before you stopped them. Tell the children to carry on with their tasks by giving the instruction 'Continue working'.

After a short while, give the 'Freeze' command. Ensure that all the children are standing still and remaining silent in their positions as zoo workers. Tap a child on the shoulder and ask the question 'What were you doing just before I froze you?' Allow the child to respond and then recycle his or her answer to the rest of the class, using tone and volume to convey the importance of the job and of the person doing it, for example:

TEACHER: What were you doing just before I froze you?
CHILD: Stacking the shelves.
TEACHER: One of the workers in the zoo shop is stacking the shelves so that the visitors will have plenty of things to buy.

Repeat this process of starting the action, freezing it and questioning children several times. Ensure that you choose the children to question carefully, selecting those who will be confident enough to be able to respond in front of the rest of the class.

After repeating this process a few times, allow the children to continue with their jobs as zoo workers. Go back into role as the zoo director and inform the children that you are returning to your office.

STAGE 2:

After a short while, leave your office and ask the children, as zoo workers, to gather together for a meeting as you have something important to tell them. Once they are seated appropriately, tell the children: *I have just received a telephone call from the zoo Head Office. Our zoo has been given some money by Head Office to spend on planting trees, shrubs and flowers in the zoo to create a zoo garden.* Then ask: *How shall we design and plan the garden?* Come out of role and gather the whole class around the display board again, ensuring that they can all see the board clearly.

Tell the children that they are all going to decide what to plant in the zoo and where trees, shrubs and flowers should be placed. Inform them that you have some suggestions for suitable plants. Show the children the pictures of trees, shrubs and flowers you have collected together and give them information about each one. Allow them to ask as many questions as they like regarding the plants – but ensure that you know the answers!

Scholastic
DRAMA
Workshop

Refer the children to the zoo plan on the display board and encourage suggestions about what should be chosen and potential positioning. Explore several possibilities: a picnic area; a woodland area; a hedgerow; a special garden containing flowers and shrubs; a pond and water garden; or the planting of flowers around the animal areas and facilities just to brighten up the zoo. Encourage the children to consider whether any specific trees, shrubs or flowers would be beneficial to, and suitable for, their own particular zoo areas, paying special attention to any plants which could either feed, or may be harmful to, their animals.

In negotiation with the children, plan your zoo garden in detail. Inform them that the garden plans have to be submitted on paper to the zoo Head Office and ask them to work with the others in their group to complete the plans. Hand out the photocopies of your drawn zoo plan, along with crayons or felt-tipped pens, and ask the children to work in their groups to draw in the idea you have just finalized. Allow a specific length of time to complete this task – between 10 and 20 minutes, depending on the age and ability level of the children. When they have completed their garden designs, collect them in and inform them, in role, that you will now submit their plans to Head Office. Ask the children to continue with their zoo jobs.

STAGE 3:
After a short while, 'return' in role from Head Office and inform the children that their zoo garden plans have been accepted. Tell them that you have brought the trees, shrubs and flowers for planting and that you would now like them to plant these in and around their zoo areas. Ask each group of children to explain what they have to do, to reinforce their acceptance of the garden planting and ensure that they are clear about what is required of them. Tell the children that you will visit each zoo area in turn to help them with their planting. Still in role as the zoo director, ask them to continue with their new jobs of planting the zoo garden.

Allow the activity to continue until the planting has been completed. Tell the children that they have all worked extremely hard and that you are very pleased with the results.

Ask the children to complete a new 'Daily report form' to record all of the work they have completed, and to make a list of the jobs they

still have to complete in their various zoo areas. When these have been completed, gathered together and filed carefully, thank the children for their efforts and inform them that the zoo is now closed.

It is at this point that some children may request transfers to different parts of the zoo. As far as is practicable, allow this to happen and consider making several job swaps.

Make sure you have incorporated the garden plan neatly and carefully into your main zoo plan on the display board.

FOLLOW-UP ACTIVITIES:
Ask the children to:
- rewrite their 'Daily report forms' (photocopiable page 143) neatly
- continue their diary of the activities completed so far, if they started a diary after activity session 1
- complete their garden plans in more detail (allow time for full colour drawings), writing the proper names of the trees, shrubs and flowers underneath each one in the plan.

PREPARATION FOR ACTIVITY SESSION 4:
Plan job swaps for the children when they are working in role, if relevant.

4
THE ZOO COMPANY IN TROUBLE

OBJECTIVES:
To highlight social responsibility and care for animals.

RESOURCES:
Completed daily report forms from previous session; photocopiable pages 143 (blank 'Daily report forms') and 144 (an enlarged copy); a

play telephone; A4 paper; list of job swaps (optional); board or flip chart; writing materials.

GROUP SIZE:
Whole group, small groups and individual participation within whole-group context.

STAGE 1:
Establish the zoo arena in the classroom, as previously. Allocate new jobs, if relevant, referring to your prepared list. Advise the children to mime putting on their work clothes, and go into role as the zoo director by miming putting on your own uniform. Tell them that you will have to have a meeting of all the zoo workers because something very sad has happened. Give the children the following news: *One of the animals (decide which one) has become seriously ill after being fed*

Scholastic
DRAMA
Workshop

something inappropriate by a member of the public visiting the zoo. The animal is being looked after in the animal hospital.

You may have made provision for an animal hospital in your zoo grounds. If not, it can be assumed that this building is sited away from the zoo.

Produce the blank enlarged 'Animal hospital report' form (photocopiable page 144) and ask the children to help you to complete it, to make a report on the problem, treatment and current status of the sick animal.

Ask the children to go to their areas and to check their own animals to see if any others are sick. Allow this activity to continue for a short while and then call all of the zoo workers together again to report back to you with their findings.

The children will respond imaginatively to your request and will either return laden with sick animals, or will assure you that no other animals are ill! You must prepare yourself for either response, reacting sympathetically to zookeepers whose animals are also sick, or being relieved that no other animals have been affected.

Advise the children that you are now going to use mime to re-create what the zoo workers saw when they went to the animal area and saw their sick animal. If no other animals are ill, ask them to imagine what they would have seen if they'd visited the area of the animal who is sick.

Nominate three or four children to mime being the animals and ask others to be the relevant zoo workers. Choose one child to portray the sick animal and encourage the children to consider how all the other animals in that area might react to it lying there ill. Ask the zoo workers and animals to show the rest of the class what they saw and did when they arrived at the animal area. Stipulate that this action should be carried out silently.

Inform the children that you are going to ask them to repeat the action, but this time you are going to 'freeze' their mime and ask them to reveal their thoughts and feelings out loud. Repeat the process of miming the zoo workers visiting their animal areas, either with the same or a different animal. At a pertinent point in the mime, give the 'Freeze' command, tap a child on the shoulder and ask him or her to speak what they are thinking or feeling aloud. Tap each child representing a zoo worker in turn and encourage them to speak their thoughts or feelings.

Gather all the zoo workers together again. Ask them what they think you should do about this terrible problem. It is hoped that at least one child will suggest reporting the problem. If not, then guide the drama by asking: *Should I telephone our Head Office?* or by saying: *I think I'd better telephone our Head Office.*

STAGE 2:

Bring in your play telephone and dial Head Office. Respond as if someone answers on the other end of the line. Now you will have to become the link between the Head Office questions and the zookeepers' responses. Establish this link by saying into the telephone: *Could you hold on just a moment while I ask them?* and then turning to the children, who are in role as zookeepers, and saying: *Head Office want to know exactly what happened, how many animals are ill and how bad they are.*

Allow the children to respond and then relay their responses to Head Office. Accept anything they say as their interpretation of events. This conversation between you, as zoo director, the Head Office and the children as zookeepers can continue for as long as you wish, and you can ask the children to respond to a number of different questions or requests from the imaginary person on the other end of the telephone to establish as much as possible about the events which have occurred.

STAGE 3:

After completing the telephone conversation, advise the children that Head Office needs an official report of what has happened at the zoo. Ask them to get back into their zoo worker groups, and write a brief outline of what has happened. Some will have been directly affected, others barely at all, but all of the zoo workers should understand what has happened and be able to record it. Gather the notes together and thank them for their assistance.

As the zoo director, ask the children if they have any suggestions for preventing this from happening again. Write on the board any suggestions given. Use these to form a basis for the last piece of work: either creating notices telling people not to feed the animals; redesigning the zoo to prevent visitors from getting close to the animals; devising a leaflet informing people of the dangers of feeding the wrong food to animals, and so on. Respond to their suggestions, ensuring that the zoo implements their valid ideas.

While the children are working on this final task, telephone the animal hospital to enquire about the sick animal(s). Inform the children that all is well and the animal(s) will make a full recovery. This is essential if children are not going to go home distressed.

FOLLOW-UP ACTIVITIES:

Ask the children to:
- complete the zoo 'Daily report forms'
- rewrite neatly their notes giving an official report to Head Office
- complete their work arising from their suggestions for preventing further problems at the zoo, carried out in stage 3 – creating notices, redesigning the zoo, devising information leaflets.

PREPARATION FOR ACTIVITY SESSION 5:

Make a certificate or choose a prize to be awarded to the children in their roles as zoo workers at the end of the project.

5

THE ZOO COMPANY
WINS A PRIZE!

OBJECTIVES:
Final problem-solving and reinforcement of subject knowledge.

RESOURCES:
Completed 'Daily report forms' from previous session; photocopiable pages 143 (blank 'Daily report forms'), 144, 145 and 146; addressed envelope for letter; prepared certificate or prize to be awarded; blank sheets of paper; writing and drawing materials.

GROUP SIZE:
Whole group, small groups and individual participation within whole-group context.

STAGE 1:
Establish the zoo setting in the classroom, as previously. Mime with the children putting on uniforms and gathering tools. When you are in role as the zoo director, allocate outstanding tasks to your zoo workers from previous daily report forms. Ensure that all children are in role as zoo workers and are focused on their tasks. When they are, inform them that you will be in your office, and 'leave' the zoo arena.

After a short while, return to the zoo arena with the important letter (photocopiable page 145) in its envelope, and tell the children that they have just received a very important letter. Gather your zoo workers together for a meeting to discuss it. Take time to look at the envelope and encourage discussion about who it could have come from, its possible contents, how important it looks, and so on. Allow this speculation to continue for a short while and build the tension as much as possible before opening the letter. It is important that this 'prop' captures the imagination of the children. Try to make it as interesting and intriguing as you possibly can.

Open the letter and show it to the children. Ask them if anyone would like to read its contents. If you have a strong reader in the class, allow him or her to read the letter aloud, if not, read it aloud yourself to the class.

Discuss the contents and encourage the excitement to grow. Emphasize the aspect of all zoo workers attending the prize-giving ceremony and wait to see if any of the children realize that this will result in the zoo and the animals being left unattended. If this doesn't occur, mention this fact yourself by saying, 'But who will look after the zoo?' Encourage the class to discuss this problem and invite suggestions and ideas from the children as to how the dilemma can be resolved. If one of the children offers to stay behind, don't allow it as this negates the whole exercise! Thank the child for the offer, but refer to the letter stating that all zoo workers should attend the award ceremony.

Introduce the possibility of another person being invited to look after the zoo while you are all at the award ceremony. Tell the children: *We need an animal expert who could look after the zoo for the time we are away and I know just the person.*

STAGE 2:

Continue with: *But this animal expert is extremely busy and so we must write as soon as we can to ask if they could come in and take care of the zoo and the animals for us.*

Give the children writing paper and pens or pencils and ask them to draft a letter to the animal expert, asking them to look after the zoo. Write a letter yourself as well.

Once this letter has been completed, gather them all in, put them in an envelope and tell the children to continue with their zoo duties while you deliver the letters to the animal expert. 'Leave' the zoo arena.

After a short while, return to the zoo and call a meeting of all the zoo workers again. Inform them that the animal expert has agreed to look after the zoo, and will even bring some other experts along to help.

Allow the children time to respond to this good news and then say: *Our expert needs to know all about our zoo jobs, what we do and how we care for our animals so that the zoo can keep going.*

Reinforce this request from the animal expert, telling the children that you think it would be a very good idea if they all completed a 'Zoo worker's duties' form (photocopiable page 146) to leave behind for the animal expert. Encourage the children to respond positively to your suggestion.

STAGE 3:

Ask the children to get together in their small groups of workers, and distribute copies of photocopiable page 146. Talk through the form first before asking the children to complete it, working together in their groups. Discuss with the children what information should be recorded and ask them to make a special note of any particular food, care or treatment their animal needs to feel happy in its environment.

Ensure you make any children working in the shop or food store feel as if they are making an important contribution to this exercise as well – their jobs are equally vital. If they complete their forms quickly, you could always ask them to assist the animal keepers.

Supervise and guide the children in their completion of these forms, acting in role as the zoo director while also ensuring that the information is factually correct and legible. Move around the classroom, helping where needed, making suggestions and asking questions to encourage the children to think carefully about the importance of ensuring that the temporary zoo workers have all the information they need. You could also include the care of the new garden – the trees, shrubs and flowers will also need to be looked after.

When the forms have been completed, discuss as many of them as possible with the children, asking for any suggestions for information which you feel may have been omitted and which may be essential to the safety and well-being of the animals, and the smooth running of the zoo. Then gather all the forms together and let the children observe you filing them away safely, ready to be handed over to the animal expert.

Finally, tell the children: *We are now going to imagine that we have been given our award and I want us to make a picture of the photograph which was taken afterwards.* Ask them to group themselves as if they were in a group photograph and encourage discussion about positioning (so that everyone can be seen) and facial expressions, (big smiles!). Stand in the photograph yourself, holding the certificate, prize or whatever you have decided shall be awarded.

Instruct the children that you are going to count to three and that on 'three' they are to freeze as if they are in the photograph. Say: *Are we all ready and in position? Good. One, two, three!* Hold the pose for a couple of seconds and then break. Thank the children for their hard work and excellent contributions and inform them that the zoo drama project has now ended.

FOLLOW-UP ACTIVITIES:

The main intention of any follow-up work at the end of this project should be to reinforce subject knowledge, while also providing opportunities to expand the use of any new skills. This could include asking the children to:

- complete their daily report forms
- write a final diary extract about attending the awards ceremony
- draw a storyboard sequence recording the award ceremony
- draw a storyboard sequence of the whole project, with short captions
- write a short piece explaining what they have learned from the project
- write a short piece about one of the animals
- find out more information about any of the aspects of the project – the countries where the animals came from; visiting a zoo; researching plants; food studies; planning a location (this could be applied to designing a school playground, for example).

ZOO ANIMAL FACT SHEET

Your name	
Animal name	
FACT 1 Country	
FACT 2 Habitat	
FACT 3 Food	
FACT 4	
FACT 5	

Scholastic
DRAMA
Workshop

DAILY REPORT FORM

Zoo worker's name:

Zoo area:

Jobs done:

Additional information:

Jobs to do:

ANIMAL HOSPITAL REPORT

Name of animal	
Name of keeper	
What is wrong with the animal?	
How did it happen?	
Treatment	

To all the members of the zoo company,

Congratulations! You have been awarded the prize of 'The best kept zoo'. This award is only given to very special zoos once a year.

We would like to award this prize to all zoo workers and your zoo director at a special ceremony at 2.00pm on Wednesday 3rd October.

The prize will be awarded by The Chief of Zoos and we are looking forward to meeting you all.

We do hope you can all attend.

Congratulations again.

With best wishes,
Yours sincerely

Mrs C Brown
Zoo Chief

ZOO WORKER'S DUTIES

Name of animal	
Name of keeper	
Temperature	
Feeding time	
Food	
Cleaning-out time	
Special jobs	
Food orders	
Buying supplies	
Other information	

Scholastic
DRAMA
Workshop

Chapter Nine

INTERPRETING HISTORY

INTRODUCTION

Project description

This project explores two historical periods through events as seen by children living in that time. The periods explored are the late Victorian years and the 1920s, giving children an opportunity to examine lifestyles in the different eras. The approach is a reflective one, with the whole project being introduced and led by a character devised and played by the teacher. This central character guides the children through their exploration of history.

Why this project?

Drama is an ideal way of enabling children to understand history, allowing them to identify with lifestyles, engage with historical concepts and understand remote and distant events by using a shared experiential process. The exploration of history through drama also encourages children to consider their own family histories.

This project combines exploring historical fact with creating historical fiction, resulting in an implicit learning process achieved through practical experience.

Length of project

Each activity session in the project, including the introductory session, is designed to be completed within 45 to 60 minutes. There are a total of four sessions, resulting in the complete project lasting approximately four hours. This could be extended, through research and supportive writing tasks, to cover a whole term's work; or the project could be completed in one week of sustained intensive work.

Project organization

The project is organized into the following sections:
- introductory session – introduces the subject context
- activity session 1 – 'Agnes introduces the Victorian years'
- activity session 2 – 'Maggie introduces the 1920s'
- activity session 3 – 'Martha's conclusion', the central character closes the project
- photocopiable resources and photographs.

Learning aims
- Subject knowledge and understanding: (history) explores history and historical change; encourages children to identify with remote lifestyles; provides a strong base for historical research; (drama) provides experience of a variety of drama conventions.
- Personal and social development: encourages children to consider their own ancestry and personal history.

Drama strategies

This project centres upon a number of practical drama methods which encourage the children to work both imaginatively and constructively in order to engage fully in the historical context. The drama conventions used allow for a wide range of progressive approaches, from individual mime, through role-playing in pairs, to whole-group improvisation. All of the sessions are focused on a central character who is a constant 'role' throughout each historical period. The teacher acts as facilitator, adopting 'role' as both an introduction to the project sessions, and during sessions to move the drama forward.

Resources needed

Factual books on the two historical periods explored in the project; photocopiable pages 158–162; 'Martha's book' – to be compiled by

Scholastic
DRAMA
Workshop

the teacher from photocopiable resources; costume items (a shawl, an apron); school hall; chairs; paper; writing and drawing materials.

What the children do

Children respond imaginatively to the teacher-in-role as the instigator of the drama and as subsequent characters within the activity sessions. They participate in a variety of drama conventions which explores each historical period through the events surrounding a central character's fictional life. Children will be expected to suspend their disbelief in order to participate fully in the imaginative experience.

What the teacher does

The teacher acts as facilitator, adopting the initial role which introduces the drama, and subsequent roles as central characters. The teacher also guides the drama by asking structured questions out of role, which facilitate the learning process for the children. The teacher should also prepare carefully for this project by researching each of the historical periods concerned, to ensure factual accuracy.

Assessment

Written evidence can be achieved through creative and structured writing exercises, both during and after the project's completion. Follow-on assignments should assess and consolidate factual knowledge. Use the assessment section of this book for recording achievements (see pages 13–20). Link assessment to the *Desirable Outcomes for Children's Learning* or KS1 level indicators.

INTRODUCTORY SESSION

Resources needed

Martha's book containing photographs and notes (made using a copy of photocopiable pages 159–162); chair; shawl; photocopiable page 158.

What to do

Ask the children to sit in a circle, or where they can all see you clearly. Tell them that you are going to tell them a very special story. Put on the shawl, sit on a chair, placed centrally, and begin to read them 'Martha's story' (photocopiable page 158). When suggested in the text, mime the actions referred to in the story. You should not worry unduly about having superb acting skills to 'perform' the role of Martha; good storytelling technique is all that is required.

After reading the story, show the children Martha's book that you have made, saying: *This is that special book.* Remain in role as 'Martha' and allow yourself to be 'hot-seated' by saying to the children: *I expect you have a lot of things you'd like to know about Martha and her book. Ask me any questions you like.* This should encourage the children to ask a wide variety of questions on different aspects of the drama, from requesting personal information about Martha and general information about the contents of the shed, to asking specific questions about the book.

Children may be a little hesitant at first, especially if the technique of hot-seating is new to them, but will soon feel confident enough to participate. Some children may repeat a question already asked – this can occur when a child wants to join in but hasn't the confidence to formulate a question – simply repeat the answer. Make sure that you prepare well in advance for the hot-seating session – have your answers ready!

Continue with the hot-seating session until you feel that the children have been given enough information for you to move the drama forward into exploring the contents of the book in more detail. Say to the children: *Martha has to go now,* removing the shawl as you do so. Come out of role and stop the drama context by turning and writing the following names and dates on the board for the children to see:

AGNES 1899   MAGGIE 1929

These refer to the photographs and notes (photocopiable pages 159–162) written in Martha's book and form the basis of the historical dramas. If you haven't already established the content of the book through the hot-seating questions, say to the children: *These names and dates are in Martha's book. Let's have a look, shall we?* If you have already established the content of the book, simply say: *Martha's book looks interesting, doesn't it? I think we should have a closer look.*

Turn to the photograph and note which refers to Agnes (photocopiable pages 159–160). Show the children the photograph and read the note out loud to them. Initiate a short question and answer session about Agnes, asking the children various questions, such as:

How old is Agnes? What does Agnes do? Does she go to school? How would you describe her clothes? What is her note about? and so on.

Repeat the same process with the other photograph and note (photocopiable pages 161–162), asking the children questions such as: *What is happening in the photograph? Which one is Maggie? What is she doing? How old is Maggie? Are any other members of her family in the photograph? Who do you think they are? What sort of clothes are the people wearing?* Help the children to explore the contents of the note, linking it to the photograph.

Try to build up a comprehensive picture of the two children mentioned in the book, but also try to leave room for further exploration. At the end of the two question and answer sessions, inform the children: *We are going to find out all about what happened to Agnes and Maggie and what their lives were like, so I'll put Martha's book somewhere safe until next time.* Thank the children for their efforts and ensure that they know that the session is at an end.

You could now ask the children to write up, or draw, the information they have gathered from this session.

Scholastic
DRAMA
Workshop

AGNES INTRODUCES THE VICTORIAN YEARS

OBJECTIVES:
To explore Victorian life through the fictional experiences of a child living at that time.

RESOURCES:
School hall; Martha's book from introductory session.

GROUP SIZE:
Whole group, small groups and individual work.

STAGE 1:
Gather the children around you so that they can all see Martha's book. Read the note from Agnes again and recap any important points raised during the discussion in the introductory session. Look at the photograph and discuss who each person might be. Take time to discuss exact positions, body language, facial expressions and so on. Ask the children to form groups of four and to re-create the photograph exactly in a freeze, advising them to pose in the same way as the people in the photograph. If the group does not divide into fours equally, ask any 'spare' children to become photographers, moving around the room and taking photographs of the groups. If you have no remaining children, perform this role yourself to encourage the groups to 'freeze'.

Ask the children to sit down where they are and tell them that they are all going to explore what Agnes and Norah did on the day when Agnes wrote her entry into Martha's book. Ask them: *What job did Agnes do at the big house before the party?* When they have given you the correct answer (sweeping and cleaning all the fire grates before lighting fires in them) instruct them to find a space to work in. Ask them to mime Agnes doing her job at the big house. Allow the mime to continue for a short while, praising and encouraging as much as possible, and then ask the children to stop working. Instruct the children to sit down where they are.

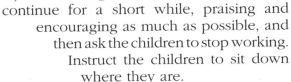

Now ask them: *What job did Norah do at the big house before the party?* (Helped the cook to prepare all the food.) Again, instruct the children to find a space to work in and then ask them all to mime Norah doing her job at the big house. Allow the mime to continue for a short while, again praising and encouraging as much as possible, and then tell the children to stop working. Finally, gather the children together to sit with you in a circle.

STAGE 2:

Continue the session with a discussion, asking the children to suggest other jobs that might have been done at the big house in preparation for the party. Suggestions could be polishing furniture, cleaning windows, cleaning and polishing cutlery, setting the table, sweeping the floors, mopping or polishing the floors, cooking the food, and so on. Allocate one of the suggested jobs to various children, either working alone, in pairs, or with two or three others.

Instruct the children to find a space to work in to do their jobs. Inform them that you will be Miss Carstairs, checking to see if they are doing their jobs properly, while they perform a whole-group role-play of the servants getting the big house ready for the party. Go into role as Miss Carstairs and say: *Right, everyone, get to work!*

Move around the room as Miss Carstairs, ensuring that the children are all 'on task'. Some children may come to you to say that they have finished their work. If they do, allocate them another task! Allow the role-play to continue until you feel that all jobs have been completed satisfactorily.

Once you have decided to end the role-play, stop the action by saying, in role: *Thank you very much. The house is now ready for the party and you may all stop work.* If some children protest that they haven't completed their tasks, simply inform them that you are happy with the job they have done and will complete it yourself later if necessary.

Come out of role and gather the children together in a circle around you again. Lead a brief discussion about what it was like for the children to work at the big house, using questions such as: *What do you think Miss Carstairs was like? Were the servants allowed to go to the party? Do you think the work was hard?* and so on. Allow the children the opportunity to ask you questions if any arise, but be prepared with the answers!

STAGE 3:

Ask the children to think about what activities Agnes and Norah might have participated in when they weren't working. What games might they have played in their leisure time? Tell the children that you want them to create photographs which show Agnes and Norah playing.

This is where factual accuracy is important. Children will happily accept being corrected if factually incorrect, providing that their contributions are acknowledged. Ensure that you are aware of which leisure pursuits are factually correct for the Victorian period!

Nominate three or four children to form a small group who will create a freeze of Agnes and Norah at play, using those ideas suggested and accepted during discussion. Guide the group in their work by asking: *What is your photograph going to show us?* Once the context of the photograph has been decided, help the children to position themselves for their photograph. Then encourage the children to create their freeze photograph by saying: *Are you all ready? All right, three, two, one, freeze!* Allow the photograph to be held for a few seconds, giving the rest of the group time to absorb the picture. Thank the small group for their efforts, nominate a new group of children, choose a new photograph context and repeat the process.

Continue creating photographs, using a different group of children each time. You will find that some of the ideas are repeated, which is perfectly acceptable as each one will look completely different. Some children may also begin to volunteer for participation, which should be positively encouraged.

Once all the suggestions have been exhausted, gather the children around you again and initiate a brief recap discussion, encouraging the children to reconsider both the working life and the leisure activities of children living in the Victorian era. A good starting point would be to ask: *What have we learned about Agnes and the way she lived?* Thank the children for their efforts and ensure that they understand that the session is now at an end.

You could inform the children at this point that the next session will explore Maggie's entry in Martha's book.

FOLLOW-UP ACTIVITIES:
Ask the children to:
• draw a day in the life of Agnes
• research the lives of children in Victorian times
• use research to create a whole-class drawing of a Victorian street scene
• devise a piece of creative writing which describes the party.

2
MAGGIE INTRODUCES THE 1920S

OBJECTIVES:
To explore life in the 1920s through the fictional experiences of a child living at that time.

RESOURCES:
School hall; Martha's book; chairs.

GROUP SIZE:
Whole group and small group work.

STAGE 1:
Sit with the children in a circle, ensuring that they can all see Martha's book. Read Maggie's note again and then look at the photograph together. Initiate a discussion about the content of the photograph, recapping the information that was established in the introductory session. Ask the children: *How do we know it was taken a long time ago? Is it*

different from photographs of weddings taken these days? What are the differences? What is the same? How many bridesmaids are there? Which person is Maggie's sister, Sally? and so on. Ask the children to make suggestions about other people in the photograph, such as who they might be, and to look carefully at exactly how they are all positioned, what their facial expressions are like, and so on. Take the time to build up as much information about the photograph as possible.

Inform the children that, as a whole group, they are going to re-create the wedding photograph. Set out a row of chairs and nominate children to sit on the chairs as the people on the front row of the photograph. Gradually nominate other children to stand behind these chairs, placing them as other people in the photograph. Try to ensure that positions and facial expressions are accurate, and take as much time as necessary to complete this. Finally, once all of the children are in position, tell them that you will now take the photograph and that, on your command of 'Freeze', they should all stand still, in silence, as they would be in the real photograph. Focus their attention by saying: *Are you all ready and in position? All right then, three, two, one, freeze!* Encourage them to hold position for a few seconds and then release them by thanking them and instructing them to sit in a circle with you again.

Ask the children to think about what other photographs might have been taken at the wedding, either before or after the one in Martha's book. Some suggestions could be: bride and groom alone, bride's family, groom's family, bridesmaids alone, bride and groom stepping out of the church door, and so on. Tell the children that you would like to see these other photographs which were taken at the wedding. Then either ask for volunteers, or nominate specific children, to create each of the photographs suggested to show to the rest of the group. Choose the correct number of people for each photograph, allocate roles and then ask them to think carefully about who they are and their positions in each photograph. After allowing a short period of time for preparation and organization, give each group a countdown and then the instruction to 'freeze'.

The main aspect to consider is how the photographs were 'staged' then; they were much more formal, less creative and the women were often seated – a throwback to the Victorian era!

Work through as many different possible photographs in this way, until all suggestions have been incorporated. Thank the children for their efforts and gather them around you in a circle again.

STAGE 2:

Now ask the children to think about the party which took place after the wedding ceremony. Ask them: *What food would they have eaten? What sort of music would have been played? What type of dancing did they do? How many guests would have been invited?* and so on.

Scholastic
DRAMA
Workshop

It is essential that you have facts prepared to correct children if they present inaccurate historical information. Much less money was spent on weddings then, and this family were obviously not rich to begin with. They will accept your corrections happily, if given in the context of building an accurate historical picture.

Once you have built a picture of what the wedding party would have been like, inform the children that you want them to pretend that you are all people at the wedding party and to act out what it would have been like. Nominate specific children to play the roles of the bride, groom and bridesmaids and allow the others to choose their own roles. Tell the children that on your count of 'three', the wedding party should begin and that when you shout 'Freeze!' the party should stop. After ensuring that all of the children are clear about their roles and what is expected of them, count to three.

You should also join in as one of the people at the wedding party. This will enable you to control the improvisation from within, ensuring that the children stay in role as much as possible.

Allow the wedding party improvisation to continue for a short while, until every child is completely absorbed and involved and then give the 'Freeze' command. Thank the children for their efforts and tell them what a good time you had at their party.

Inform them that you would now like to see a photograph of the bride and groom leaving the party with everybody else waving goodbye. Nominate certain children to portray specific roles in the photograph and ask for suggestions about positioning, facial expressions, grouping, and so on. When all preparation is complete, give the children a countdown from three and then instruct them to all 'freeze!' Hold the photograph pose for a few seconds, then thank the children for their efforts and ask them to sit in a circle with you again.

STAGE 3:

Initiate a final discussion which focuses on Maggie's involvement in the wedding. Encourage the children to consider how the day was for Maggie by asking such questions as: *Was Maggie excited about the wedding? What was Maggie's favourite part of the day? How did Maggie feel after it was all over? Who would Maggie have talked to about how she was feeling?* This last question should prompt the children to consider the relationship between Maggie and her sister, Sally, who was also a bridesmaid.

Now ask the children to think specifically about what Maggie and Sally would have talked about that evening, when the wedding was all

over, and what they would have said to each other. Tell them that you want them to make up and act out the conversation between Maggie and Sally that night. Ask the children to find a partner and a space to work in and tell them to decide which of them will be Maggie and which Sally. Instruct them to start their conversations by saying: *Now imagine that you are Maggie and Sally talking all about the wedding that night. Off you go.* Move around the room, monitoring the conversations and helping any children who may be having problems getting started – this can be done by simple prompting, using the same questions as before.

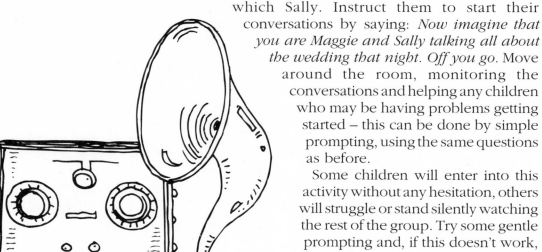

Some children will enter into this activity without any hesitation, others will struggle or stand silently watching the rest of the group. Try some gentle prompting and, if this doesn't work, leave them to observe – they'll gain just as much from doing that.

Allow the improvisation to continue for a few moments and then ask the children to stop. Thank them for their efforts and gather them into a circle again.

Finally, lead a brief recap discussion about Maggie by asking: *What have we learned about Maggie and the way she lived?* Allow the discussion to continue for a short while, then thank them again for their contributions and ensure that they understand that the session is now at an end.

FOLLOW-UP ACTIVITIES:
• Work with the children on researching the 1920s.
Ask the children to:
• bring in modern wedding photographs and compare them with the 1920s wedding
• create their own wedding photo using drawn pictures of other members of the class
• draw a picture of the wedding party
• draw a picture of one of the other wedding photographs they created
• write a description of the wedding.

3

MARTHA'S CONCLUSION

OBJECTIVES:
Using the initial character to close the project.

RESOURCES:
Martha's book; chair; shawl; paper; writing and drawing materials.

GROUP SIZE:
Whole group and individual work.

Scholastic
DRAMA
Workshop

STAGE 1:

Sit on the chair and make sure the children are sitting where they can see Martha's book clearly. Go straight into role as Martha by putting on the shawl and saying: *It was really interesting learning all about the people in my book, wasn't it? What did you enjoy the most?* Allow the children to respond, taking answers from as many as possible. Then say: *I'd like to be in the book myself. Will you draw a picture of me to put in the book while I write my note?* The answer should be affirmative from all of the children! Give out some drawing paper and crayons for the children to draw a picture of Martha.

While the children are drawing, write your note on an A4 piece of paper. It should read: *Today when I was tidying up the garden shed, I found a very interesting book with photographs and notes in it about people who lived a long time ago. These people were called Agnes and Maggie and I learned all about them and the way they used to live.*

Come out of role by removing the shawl and putting the book down. Once the children have finished their drawings of Martha, collect them in and keep them safe to use in a display with Martha's note.

STAGE 2:

Distribute more sheets of drawing paper and ask the children to draw a picture of their favourite character from Martha's book, writing the name of that character underneath their picture.

When these have all been completed, ask each child to come to the front of the classroom, show their picture to the rest of the class and explain who it is and why they liked that person the best.

STAGE 3:

Work with the class as a whole group to recall verbally the sequence of events during the project, from Martha's first appearance to her final one. Encourage the children to remember everything which occurred during the project and all the activities in which they participated.

If you want to create a storybook (see follow-up activities below), it would be a good idea to make a note of the sequences of events as discussed by the group.

Thank the children for their contributions and ensure that they all understand that the project is now at an end.

FOLLOW-UP ACTIVITIES:

As a class:
• create a storybook about the whole project, with pictures and illustrative sentences
• continue with the research into the two different historical periods.

Ask the children to:
• draw their own picture and write their own notes for inclusion in Martha's book.

Martha lived all alone in a little house just off the main street. She had lived there for years and years and years – as long as she could remember.

One cold autumn day, Martha decided to have a go at clearing out the garden shed. She had left it for a very long time and knew that there was all kinds of rubbish in it which should have been sorted out years ago. The shed was meant to be full of garden tools and packets of seeds, but Martha knew that there were old toys, books and clothes in there from a very long time ago. They had all belonged to people in Martha's family.

(Mime sweeping the leaves from around the shed and opening the shed door as you read the next section.)

Martha swept the dead leaves away from the shed door and opened it slowly. She was surprised to see so many things stored inside the shed, all dusty and dirty, and decided to have a good tidy up.

(Mime dusting the items in the shed as you read this next section.)

Martha was busily sorting and dusting when she suddenly noticed an old wooden box in the corner of the shed. On the side of the box she could just make out the painted letters 'ABC'. Martha was puzzled. She couldn't remember seeing the box before. What was it? Who had it belonged to? When had it been put in the garden shed? "How strange!" she thought.

(Mime finding the box, opening it and finding the book.)

Martha cleared a space and pulled the box out. It was quite heavy and obviously very old. The lock on the front had been broken. The lid was a bit stiff but Martha managed to lift it. She peered inside…
Books! Red, blue, yellow and green books, leather-bound books with photographs, books with drawings, tiny books with old writing, books that smelled a bit!

Then, at the very bottom of the box, under some old papers… Martha found a very special book.

(Produce 'Martha's book' which you have created.)

Agnes 1899
aged 10 (standing)

Today I have been helping at the big house. Mrs Cooper, the mistress of the house, is having a big party and we all helped to get everything ready. My sister, Norah, worked there too. I swept and cleaned all the fire grates and then I lit a fire in each one. I got very dirty. Norah said I was lucky – she had to help Cook to prepare the food, and her hands were nearly raw from all the washing and peeling and chopping.

Miss Carstairs, the housekeeper, kept coming in to make sure I was working hard. She shouted orders to everyone. I just tried to do my work and keep out of her way because she can be nasty when she's in a bad mood and may give us girls a beating for no good reason!

When I got home I was very tired. Mother had baked some little cakes for our tea. Norah said she couldn't eat a thing. She'd had enough of food for one day! But Mother made her eat something, anyway. The photographs have arrived from the photographic studio. We all agreed that Father looked very smart in his uniform. I was sad that my new hair ribbons didn't show up very well because they looked lovely when I put them on. I was so tired that I went to bed straight after tea, nearly an hour before I usually do.

Scholastic
DRAMA
Workshop

MAGGIE

Sally
aged 8

Maggie 1929
aged 10

MAGGIE (AGED 10)

Today was my Aunt Lillian's wedding. I was a bridesmaid, and so was my little sister, Sally. We both wore lovely white dresses with frilly collars, and flowers in our hair. Aunt Lillian's new husband, Uncle Jimmy, looked ever so smart and his hair was all shiny.

Lots of people came. All the men wore flowers in their buttonholes, and the women dressed up in their best frocks. There were eight bridesmaids including me and Sally, but the grown-up ones aren't called bridesmaids, I think they're called maids of honour.

We had a big party afterwards at the church hall. There was lots of food and dancing and singing. When Aunt Lillian and Uncle Jimmy went off in their car, we all waved and shouted goodbye. Aunt Lillian threw her bunch of flowers for someone to catch, so I threw mine as well. It hit my cousin Peter on the head! I got a real telling-off.

Scholastic
DRAMA
Workshop

Chapter Ten

STORYTELLING AND MAKING

INTRODUCTION

Project description

This project is concerned with children developing skills and expertise in storytelling and making, moving from the familiar contexts of stories already known, to devising original ideas. The approach focuses mainly on the verbal creation of fiction, although the project also includes opportunities for a substantial amount of creative and structured writing. The majority of sessions are centred upon a whole-group approach, with individual participation being encouraged rather than enforced.

Why this project?

This project allows children the shared experience of negotiating, planning and creating fictional stories and texts, providing creative learning opportunities within a supportive and encouraging environment. It enables children to use their imagination freely and to make individual contributions to a whole-group experience. The project engages the children both intellectually and emotionally and empowers them with the ability to direct the work within a structured context. Learning and development occurs gradually, as confidence builds once the children realize that all responses are valid and will be accepted without question by the teacher.

Length of project

Each activity session in the project, including the introductory session, is designed to be completed within 45 to 60 minutes. There are a total of five sessions, resulting in the project lasting approximately five hours. This could be extended, through linking creative writing and follow-on work, to cover a whole term's work; or the project could be completed in one week of intensive work.

Project organization

The project is organized into six different sections:
- introductory session – introducing the subject context
- activity session 1 – 'The broken toy'
- activity session 2 – 'Creating stories through sounds and actions (1)'
- activity session 3 – 'Creating stories through sounds and actions (2)'
- activity session 4 – 'What happened next?'
- photocopiable resources.

Learning aims

- Communication skills: develops speaking and listening skills; encourages pertinent questions and appropriate responses.
- Subject knowledge and understanding: (English) allows children to understand story construction; provides opportunities for structured and creative writing; enables children to develop verbal creativity; (drama) provides experience of various drama conventions.

Drama strategies

The drama conventions used to explore stories are very simple, ranging from whole-group role-play through to basic mime and small group freezes. The teacher is instrumental in guiding and leading the creative process by using such methods as teacher-in-role and being placed on the 'hot-seat' to respond to questions in role as a particular character.

Resources needed

A tape recorder and a supply of blank cassette tapes is essential to record each session; storybooks to provide a stimulus for creativity; text extracts (see resources in individual sessions); a hat; a broken toy (a doll with an arm or leg missing, or a broken car or similar would work well); a large ruler to use for group story-making exercise; paper; writing and drawing materials; use of the school hall for activity sessions 2 and 3; chair for 'hot-seating'.

What the children do

Children are encouraged to create stories through discussion, negotiation, questioning and providing imaginative responses. They are asked to define roles and characters and establish imaginative story contexts for those characters, exploring motives, actions and reactions to develop a structured storyline. Much of the work is completed with the children responding 'as themselves' but they will occasionally be asked to respond in role as one or more of the characters from the story.

What the teacher does

The teacher acts as facilitator and guide, encouraging appropriate responses from the

Scholastic
DRAMA
Workshop

children through questions and by leading discussions. It is essential that the teacher is sure about the objectives of each lesson and prepared to direct the children into achieving those objectives.

The teacher must encourage children to contribute by using positive responses and ensuring that the children recognize that they will not be ridiculed or ignored. While guiding the creative process, the teacher will be required to respond in role both within the context of a drama, and externally as a character on the 'hot-seat', being prepared to respond directly to questions from the children.

Assessment

Use the tape-recorded sessions as evidence of the learning development and the subject knowledge and skills gained. Written evidence will be contained in the creative and structured writing tasks. Follow-on assignments should reinforce skills and knowledge and provide an assessment of story construction. Use the assessment section of this book for recording achievements (see pages 13–20). Link assessment to the *Desirable Outcomes for Children's Learning* or KS1 level indicators.

INTRODUCTORY SESSION

Resources needed

Tape recorder and blank cassette; a familiar story, to have in mind, for instance *Cinderella*; a hat; a large ruler to use as a 'speaker's ruler'.

What to do

Sit with the children in a circle, and start recording. Inform them that you are all going to tell the story of (insert your chosen story name here). Explain that you are going to start the story and then nominate volunteers to continue, until you have told the whole story. Try to ensure that every aspect of the story is covered – and in sequence.

Nominating children, rather than asking for volunteers, ensures that all children are listening carefully becuase they may be chosen. Begin with the most confident and able children, but nominate one or two with less confidence as well, to provide encouragement.

Once you have completed your chosen well-known story, inform the children that they are now going to make up their own story. Tell them: *Everyone in the class is going to tell one part of the story.* Introduce the 'speaker's ruler'. Explain its use: *When you have the ruler it is your turn for your part of the story.* Each child takes it in turn to speak, passing the ruler to their neighbour when they have finished. No one must speak unless they have the ruler, but all must listen very carefully to the speaker.

Begin the story yourself by saying: *Once upon a time there was a very unhappy pig. He lived all alone in the pigsty in Farmer Jackson's field and spent his day eating and sleeping. One day, Farmer Jackson came to the pig and said...* Now pass the ruler to the child on your left or right to continue the story. Repeat this process all around the circle, continuing to pass the ruler around until you feel that the story has reached a natural conclusion.

Prepare for hesitations at first but, by encouraging all contributions, children should become more confident in their responses. The story will probably be quite short and is likely to end with the last child in the circle speaking, which is perfectly acceptable.

Praise the children for their efforts and say: *That was a good story, wasn't it?* Inform the children that they are now going to make up a story about a particular character. Bring out the hat you have chosen and build a comprehensive picture of its owner by asking the children questions, for example: *Who would wear this hat? How old do you think the owner is? What does the hat's owner do for a living? Is the owner of this hat rich or poor? Has the hat been lost? How often does the owner wear it? Is it a special hat?* Remember to praise all contributions, but define those which will provide a strong basis for your group story.

Tell the children that you are all now going to tell the story of the hat and its owner by passing the hat around the circle. Advise them that each child should contribute to the story by placing the hat on his or her head while they speak and then passing it on. Begin the story yourself by wearing the hat and giving an appropriate sentence which introduces the character you have all devised and the story outline. Pass the hat on to the child on your right or left. Continue this process around the circle until every child has worn the hat, given their contribution and the story has been completed. Praise their efforts, switch off the tape recorder and tell the children that the storytelling session has now ended.

THE BROKEN TOY

OBJECTIVES:
To explore the concepts of character and motive within the story context.

RESOURCES:
Tape recorder and blank cassette; a suitable broken toy; chair; a large sheet of paper; photocopiable page 106; writing materials.

GROUP SIZE:
Individual participation within whole group.

STAGE 1:
Sit with the children in a circle and start recording. Show them the broken toy and initiate a discussion about the toy by asking questions such as: *Who does the toy belong to? How did the toy get broken? Who broke the toy and why?* (The person who broke it may not be the same as the one who owns it.) *Is it a special, or a favourite, toy? Can it be mended? How does the person who broke it feel? How does the person who owns it feel?* and so on. Prepare as many questions as possible for the children to respond to, in order to build up a comprehensive story surrounding the toy.

Expand this initial discussion into developing a full chronological plot, clearly outlining events, defining and naming characters and exploring their actions and motives. In negotiation with the children, complete the full story in written form on a large sheet of paper and display this as a reference point for the children to use in stage 2. (*Note:* you can stop recording at this point, but it is advisable to leave the tape to record continuously. This will ensure a complete record of the session as well as allowing the children to forget about being recorded, so that they respond naturally, without being distracted by the tape recorder being switched on and off.)

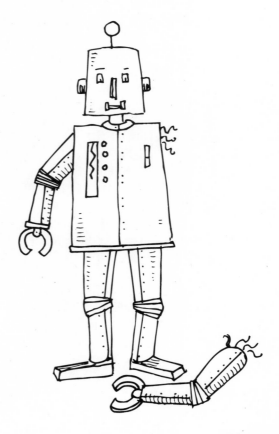

STAGE 2:
Inform the children that they are now going to tell the story from the viewpoint of the three central characters. Lead a discussion with the children to explore who the three main characters in the story are.
These will be:
- the child who has broken the toy
- the parent of the child who has broken the toy
- the toy-maker who tries to mend the toy.

Scholastic
DRAMA
Workshop

Inform the children that, using the chronological plot written on the large sheet of paper as a reference point, you will begin each part of the story which refers to one of these central characters and will nominate children to continue the story from that viewpoint. Give an introductory sentence for each character's story, for example:

- *Sally felt so angry as she ripped the doll's leg off...*
- *Mrs Brown sighed deeply and said, 'I just don't understand you, Sally...'*
- *The toy-maker scratched his head and said to himself, 'I can't mend this. What shall I do...?'*

Nominate children to continue each specific aspect of the story from a particular character's viewpoint, asking as many children as possible around the class to give a brief contribution. To help the children if they are struggling, take the toy back and continue the story yourself before passing it on again for the next child to speak. Once the story has been completed, discuss the characters, their actions and reactions again and make any additional notes on the large sheet of paper with the story outline on it.

STAGE 3:
Tell the children that they are now going to be given the opportunity to ask these characters questions, to see if they can gather any additional information. Bring the 'hot-seat' chair forward and inform the children of its magic powers – that when anyone sits on this hot-seat, they can become a different person, and especially characters from a story. Sit on the hot-seat and tell the children that you are now one of the characters from the story (you decide which one to nominate first). Ask the children for their questions and answer them in role.

You must visibly become the character you have chosen by altering your body language, facial expression and vocal expression, but be careful not to caricature too much or the children's belief will be lost. Sustain your role throughout all of the questions, and answer as you think the character would.

Once you have completed this process of hot-seating one character, leave the chair to lead a discussion with the children on what you have discovered about that character. Add this information to the large sheet of paper. Then sit back down in the chair, go into role as another character and repeat the exercise. After each question and answer session with a character from the story, add any further information to the sheet of paper until you have built up a story outline with defined characters who reveal a comprehensive set of emotions, motives, actions and reactions. Repeat the exercise as often as required – before the children become obviously bored with the process!

Thank the children for their efforts and reinforce their learning process by saying: *Well, we have learned a lot about these characters in our story, haven't we? I think we know them so well now that they almost seem real, don't they?* Ensure that the children understand that the session is completed.

FOLLOW-UP ACTIVITIES:
Ask the children to:
- draw a picture of each of the characters in the story, and write one or two descriptive sentences underneath each picture
- use the storyboard (photocopiable page 106) to draw a series of pictures in sequence that show the whole story – captions could also be added underneath each frame
- write the story in detail.

Invite confident, willing children to:
- take the hot-seat as other characters – question them yourself about their involvement in the story.

PREPARATION FOR ACTIVITY SESSION 2:
Choose a familiar story to tell or read to the children. Pick one that has a potential for sound effects and mime. Rewrite the story created in this session, using the chronological plot on the paper and the tape-recording, for use in activity session 4.

2
CREATING STORIES THROUGH SOUNDS AND ACTIONS (1)

OBJECTIVES:
Using sound effects and actions to explore story settings.

RESOURCES:
School hall; tape recorder and blank cassette; text of familiar story, for instance *Little Red Riding Hood*, *The Three Billy Goats Gruff*, *The Three Little Pigs* or similar.

GROUP SIZE:
Whole group and large groups.

STAGE 1:
Sit in a circle with the children and start the tape recorder. Inform them that you are all going to make different sound effects. Start off asking all the children to make the sound of wind rushing through the trees. Allow this to continue for a few moments. Stop them and praise their efforts. Now ask the children to make the sound of rain falling on the ground. (This could be done by clicking fingers or tapping fingers on the floor.)

Work through the making of various sound effects with the children, for example someone eating an ice-cream, a dog barking, a door creaking open, a door slamming shut, a telephone ringing, a police car siren, footsteps on a pathway, someone eating cereal, a busy road, playground noises and so on. Add as many others as you wish and ask the whole group to 'perform' each sound effect together. You could choose sound effects to match the story you have selected. Some children will become very  noisy during this exercise, but a simple finger to your lips to encourage them to 'sssh' will generally quieten them down!

Work through all of the sound effects, praising their efforts constantly. Finally, ask the children for suggestions of any other sound effects they would like to try and make. You may find that one or two children will make silly, or rude, suggestions here! If they do, just let them know that their contributions are not appropriate.

Continue with this exercise until you have experimented with creating a variety of different sounds and atmospheres.

STAGE 2:
Tell the children that they are now going to create the sound effects for a story you are going to tell them, and advise them that they should listen carefully to the story as you tell/read it. Then read or tell them a short version of a familiar story. At the end of this initial read through, ask the children to consider and suggest all the different sounds which could be created from the story. Give them an example to help them to understand the concept: if you are using the story of Little Red Riding Hood, what sounds would be heard as she walked through the woods? How could we hear the door to the cottage opening? And so on. Work in sequence through the story you are using.

Instruct the children that you are going to read the story again, and that you want them to perform the sound effects they suggested to accompany the story as you read it. Ensure that all the children understand what is expected of them.

Read the story through again, pausing regularly to allow the children to create the accompanying appropriate sound effects. Continue with this process until you have completed the story reading and the children have performed all of the relevant sound effects. Praise their efforts.

STAGE 3:
Inform the children that they are now going to bring the story to life using sound and action. Tell them that you are going to read the story again and give half of the class the task to act out the story without using sounds or words – that is, to mime it; and ask the remaining half of the class to provide sound effects which support both the actions and the text.

Divide your class into two groups and place them on opposite sides of the hall, with you standing in the centre. Tell one group that they should mime all the actions as you read them, and the other group that they should provide the sound effects for the actions. None of the children providing sound effects should use dialogue – this should only be read by you.

Ensure that the children understand what is expected of them and inform the children miming the actions that as they will become all the characters, they can move around the hall as they wish. Begin reading the story for the third and final time. Read very slowly to enable those miming to complete actions and those children providing sound effects to accompany them. Continue with this process, pausing as often and for as long as is necessary, until you have completed the final story reading.

Gather the children together in a circle again, praise their efforts and ask for their reflections on what they have just achieved: how they felt about the exercise, what they found difficult, what else they could have done/added to improve their contribution, whether they enjoyed it, and so on. Ask the children for suggestions of other stories which could be explored in the same way and encourage them to reflect particularly on how sound and actions can bring a story to life. Ensure that the children understand that the session is now over. Switch off the tape recorder, if you haven't already done so.

FOLLOW-UP ACTIVITIES:
As a class:
• Use or make musical instruments to create sound effects – for the story you have used in this session or another familiar story.
• Pick several sound effects and build a story around them.
Ask the children to:
• produce a written record of this session.

Scholastic
DRAMA
Workshop

CREATING STORIES THROUGH SOUNDS AND ACTIONS (2)

OBJECTIVES:
To explore building stories using sound and action.

RESOURCES:
School hall; tape recorder and blank cassette; photocopiable pages 175 and 176.

GROUP SIZE:
Whole group, small group.

STAGE 1:
Sit with the children in a circle, start the tape recorder and guide them in a discussion which recaps the exercise they completed in the previous session. Inform them that they are now going to experience something similar, but with an unknown story.

Hand out copies of the text extract (photocopiable pages 175 and 176) so that each child can see one. Read the text through while the children follow it. Then discuss the different sound effects in the story, exploring each sound as it appears in the context of the text.

As a whole group, encourage the children to practise each sound effect, working through the story until all have been rehearsed.

STAGE 2:
Tell the children that they are now going to provide the sound effects in the story while you read it through. Advise them to remember how they decided each sound effect should sound and to listen carefully while you read.

Read the story again, pausing while the children provide the appropriate sound effects as a whole group. Continue with this process of reading, pausing and providing sound effects until the story is completed.

Praise their efforts. Inform

the children that they are now going to bring the story to life with both sounds and actions, as they did with the story in the previous session. Lead a discussion with the children, asking for suggestions for miming actions in the story and encouraging one or two children to give physical examples of the actions, for example someone eating a bowl of cereal, walking in the wind and rain, splashing through puddles, and so on. This exploration of corresponding actions could be done as a whole-group exercise, with every child miming each action.

STAGE 3:

Now divide the class into two groups, with you standing between them. Explain to one group that will be making the sound effects for the story, and tell the remaining group that they are to perform the actions for the story. Tell both groups that they must listen carefully to you while you read the story and to follow the text closely.

Inform the children who are miming the actions that they can move around the hall as they wish. Ensure that all the children understand what is expected of them. Begin reading the story for the third and final time, pausing to allow the children miming to perform the actions and those creating the sound effects to make the appropriate noises. Continue with the process until you have 'performed' the full story. Ask the children to sit in a circle again, and praise their efforts.

If the children request it – and they might – you could allow the two groups to swap, so that those performing the sound effects now mime the actions, and vice versa. Do this before bringing the children back to sit in a circle.

Ask the children to reflect on their achievements: how realistic their sound effects were, how they felt about the exercise, what they thought they'd done well, what they felt they could have done better, and so on. Discuss how using sound and action makes a difference to a story, noting whether it makes the story easier to understand or remember. Thank the children for their efforts and ensure that they understand that the session is now over.

Because they may be curious, inform the children that you will be exploring 'what happens next' in the story during the following session.

FOLLOW-UP ACTIVITIES:

Ask the children to:
- form small groups and write their own short stories
- use these stories as a basis for repeating the exercise
- perform a short story using actions only
- produce a written record of this session
- write a written account of their own journeys to school, including all sound effects (use these to repeat the exercise).

4

WHAT HAPPENED NEXT?

OBJECTIVES:
To explore story structure by devising alternative endings.

RESOURCES:
Tape recorder and blank cassette; copies of short story text (photocopiable pages 175 and 176) used in previous session; storyboard (photocopiable page 106); the rewritten 'Broken toy' story from activity session 1; flip chart or board; paper; writing materials.

GROUP SIZE:
Whole group, small group.

STAGE 1:
Ask the children to sit in their classroom places. Start the tape recorder. Hand out copies of the short story text used in the previous session (photocopiable pages 175 and 176). Read the story through, with the children following the text. Ask the children if anything has been

omitted from the story. You may get several different suggestions, all of them valid and worthy of a positive response, but at least one child should mention the fact that there is no definite ending to the story, that it has been left on a 'cliffhanger'.

Continue the discussion, exploring different options for what could have happened next. Use questions to elicit suggestions and ensure that all responses are praised. In negotiation with the children, choose a definite ending which the whole group is happy with.

You could write the various suggestions, and the final decided outcome, on the board as a reference.

STAGE 2:
Ask the children to listen to a story you are going to tell them and then read to them the 'Broken toy' story they devised in activity session 1. Ask the children: *Do any of you recognize that story?* Confirm that it is their own story creation and inform the children that you would like them to finish the story off now and write an ending for it. Organize the children into small working groups and give out pens or pencils and writing paper.

While the children are getting settled, write the story so far on the board for them to use as a prompt, and to clarify exactly where they have to continue the story from. Ask the children to follow as you read the story from the board.

Lead a very short discussion with the children, asking for suggestions on 'What happened next?' Remember to praise all contributions, as all ideas are valid. Write their suggestions for endings on a different part of the board, as a memory aid or prompt for the children.

Instruct the children to work in their small groups on writing an ending for the story. Allow a specified length of time for the writing of the story endings – between 10 and 20 minutes. Move around the room monitoring their writing, ensuring that they are including sufficient information and considering the structure in order to make the endings coherent.

STAGE 3:
Gather the finished stories together. Inform the children that their stories are now going to be read aloud and that the whole group will appraise and discuss the different endings offered. Now either read the stories yourself, ask for volunteers from each group to read them aloud or nominate readers.

Pause after each story reading and lead a whole-group discussion which considers the different endings for the story. Remember to praise and encourage all contributions. For any pieces of work which are incomplete, negotiate an outcome with the children as a whole group. Some of the writers may try to clarify exactly where their story was intending to end; accept this notion, but reinforce the fact that many stories can have many different endings and that each possibility is as valid as the next. Ensure that children do not feel that you are negating their ideas.

Once you have read and discussed each story, and finalized the ending if necessary, thank the children for their efforts and ensure that they are aware that the project is now at an end.

FOLLOW-UP ACTIVITIES:
Ask the children to:
• write the ending for the original text extract, completing it in any way they choose, or using earlier suggestions
• use the storyboard (photocopiable page 106) to draw sequential pictures of the original text extract and to continue it using pictures.
As a class:
• repeat these exercises with their own stories.

Scholastic
DRAMA
Workshop

DOUGLAS'S DAY

"Douglas!" *(pause)* "Douglas!" *(pause)* "It's time for school," called Douglas's dad. "I'll just get the phone!" **(Sound)** Douglas was watching breakfast television and eating his cereal. **(Sound)** He watched the last little bit of the programme **(Sound)** and then he turned the television off. **(Sound)**

Outside a dog barked. **(Sound)** It was Mrs Brown's dog, Mutt. It was always barking and sometimes growled. **(Sound)** Douglas put his hand in his dad's hand, pulled his hood up because it was so windy, and they stepped out of the front door.

It was so windy the door banged shut behind them. **(Sound)** It was blowing a

Scholastic
DRAMA
Workshop

gale! *(Sound)* And throwing it down with rain. *(Sound)*

"Come on, Doug," said Dad. "We'll walk quickly and be at school in no time. Watch out for the puddles!" Douglas plonked his wellies into every puddle he could see! *(Sound)* But they had to be careful when they reached the road, because it was very, very busy! *(Sound)* Soon Douglas and his dad could hear the distant sounds of other children arriving at school. *(Sound)*

Suddenly a police car came round the corner, its lights on and the siren blaring loudly. *(Sound)* "Oh, my goodness," said Dad, "just look over there!"

Scholastic
DRAMA
Workshop